MAIN ECONOMIC POLICY AREAS OF THE EEC — TOWARD 1992

International Studies in Economics and Econometrics

VOLUME 20

2782065

Main Economic Policy Areas of the EEC — Toward 1992

The Challenge to the Community's Economic Policies when the 'Real' Common Market is Created by the End of 1992

edited by

Peter Coffey
University of St. Thomas, St. Paul, Minnesota, U.S.A.

Third Revised Edition

KLUWER ACADEMIC PUBLISHERS
DORDRECHT / BOSTON / LONDON

Library of Congress Cataloging-in-Publication Data

Main economic policy areas of the EEC, toward 1992 : the challenge to
  the Community's economic policies when the "real" Common Market is
  created by the end of 1992 / edited by Peter Coffey. -- 3rd rev. ed.
      p.   cm. -- (International studies in economic and econometrics
  ; v. 20)
    Includes index.
    ISBN 0-7923-0810-7 (U.S. : alk. paper)
    1. European Economic Community countries--Economic policy.
    2. Agriculture and state--European Economic Community countries.
    3. Industry and state--European Economic Community countries.
    4. Fiscal policy--European Economic Community countries.
    5. Regional planning--European Economic Community countries.
    6. Energy policy--European Economic Community countries.
    7. Monetary policy--European Economic Community countries.
    8. Europe 1992.   I. Coffey, Peter. II. Series.
  HC241.2.M2374 1990
  337.1'42--dc20   90-4680

ISBN 0-7923-0810-7

Published by Kluwer Academic Publishers,
P.O. Box 17, 3300 AA Dordrecht, The Netherlands.

Kluwer Academic Publishers incorporates
the publishing programmes of
D. Reidel, Martinus Nijhoff, Dr W. Junk and MTP Press.

Sold and distributed in the U.S.A. and Canada
by Kluwer Academic Publishers,
101 Philip Drive, Norwell, MA 02061, U.S.A.

In all other countries, sold and distributed
by Kluwer Academic Publishers Group,
P.O. Box 322, AH Dordrecht, The Netherlands.

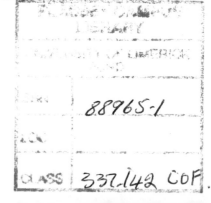

Table of contents

vi

Other books by Peter Coffey

European Monetary Integration (with John R. Presley). Macmillan, London, 1971.

The Social Economy of France. Macmillan, London, 1973.

The World Monetary Crisis. Macmillan, London and St. Martin's Press, New York, 1974.

The External Economic Relations of the EEC. Macmillan, London and St. Martin's Press, New York, 1976.

Europe and Money. Macmillan and St. Martin's Press, New York, 1977.

Economic Policies of the Common Market. Macmillan, London and St. Martin's Press, New York, 1979.

The Common Market and its International Economic Policies. The Hague, 1982.

The Main Economic Policy Areas of the EEC, (editor). Martinus Nijhoff Publishers, Den Haag, 1983.

The European Monetary System — Past, Present and Future. Martinus Nijhoff Publishers, Dordrecht, 1984; Second Edition, 1986.

The European Community and Mexico, edited, M. S. Wionczek (co-editor). Martinus Nijhoff Publishers, Dordrecht, 1987.

Towards a European Foreign Policy, edited, R. H. Lauwaars and J. K. De Vree (joint editors). Martinus Nijhoff Publishers, Dordrecht, 1987.

Europe and the Andean Countries, together with Ciro Angarita. Frances Printer, London, 1988.

The EEC and Brazil, together with L. A. Corrèa de Lago. Frances Printer, London, 1988.

The EEC and the Netherlands — Costs and Benefits together with Menno Wolters. Frances Printer, London, 1990.

Preface to the third edition

PETER COFFEY

Since the appearance of the second edition of this work — which was so quickly out of print — so much has happened in Europe. In the EEC itself, 1989 was a watershed year concerning the Community's moves towards the creation of the Single European Market (SEM) by the end of 1992. Early in the year, the appearance of the Delors Report on Economic and Monetary Union in the European Community, was followed by an agreement, at the European Summit, in June, to begin the first stage of this union in the Summer of 1990. As a counterpart to this and other agreements, seen by trade unions and similar groups as an agreement

* New composition of the ECU as on 21st September 1989.

DEM	: 30.10%	Deutsche Mark
FRF	: 19.00%	French Franc
GBP	: 13.00%	Pound Sterling
ITL	: 10.15%	Italian Lira
NLG	: 9.40%	Dutch Guilder
BFR	: 7.90%	Belgian Franc
DKK	: 2.45%	Danish Kronor
IEP	: 1.10%	Irish Pund
GRD	: 0.80%	Greek Drachma
ESP	: 5.30%	Spanish Peseta
PTE	: 0.80%	Portuguese Escudo

between governments and businesses, there followed calls for and the adoption by eleven Heads of State of a Social Charter.

But, it was towards the end of 1989 that so many other agreements were made, some of which could have far-reaching consequences in relation to 1992. After some seventeen years of discussion, agreement was finally reached on a directive for mergers. Of equal or even greater importance was the acceptance by the Ministers of the second banking directive. Then, after much heated discussion, a compromise was reached on the future margins of difference for the value added tax (VAT).

If these agreements inside the EEC were important, the events in Eastern Europe were largely unexpected, swift and potentially very far-reaching in their implications — both economic and political. The most important development concerning the Community's move towards 1992 are the proposals for German unification. Here, the plan for a monetary union between the two Germanies will have implications for the European Monetary System (EMS) and the future development of an economic and monetary union (EMU).

Despite all these changes, agreements and events, the fundamental aims and operation of the main economic policies of the EEC do remain the same as before. In some cases, notably in the area of fiscal integration, and despite the compromise reached on the VAT, little progress has been made regarding the major goals as described by the late Alan Prest and by Walter Hahn. Agricultural policy also remains very much the same as before. The EMS, with the exception of the entry of the Portuguese Escudo and the Spanish Peseta into the ECU* and the entry of Spain as an active member of the EMS in the second half of 1989 and the mini-devaluation of the Italian lira and the narrowing of the margin of fluctuation in the 'GRID' exchange mechanism from 6 to 2.25 per cent, in January, this year, remains very much as before. The same can be said for the energy and regional policies, though, regarding the latter, and, also for social policy, Community spending is being doubled between 1989 and 1993. Only in the fields of mergers' legislation and the second banking directive can one talk of a fundamental change of policy. Consequently, the authors decided, with some exceptions, to leave most of the original chapters as they were in the second edition. However, it was also agreed to analyse the details of the agreements reached inside the EEC in 1989 and the influence of events in Eastern Europe on the Community in this preface, it is to this analyses that we shall now turn.

The three decisions which could have the greatest potential influence on trade, investment and business within the EEC and between the Community and third parties concern mergers, taxation and banking. The new EEC Regulation on Preliminary Control of European Mergers, which will come into effect on 21st September 1990, is aimed not only at the control of important mergers between companies based exclusively inside the EEC but equally at those between enterprises inside and outside the Community. Indeed, only one of the two partners need to be inside the Common Market whilst total turnover of the prospective merged companies is the world wide one.

Much discussion took place between protagonists who wanted a lower threshold for turnover and those who preferred a higher one. In the event, the compromise reached was a "combined worldwide turnover for the companies concerned of at least 5 billion ECU"; such proposed mergers automatically fall within the control of the Commission to which body prior notification must be given. This threshold level will be re-examined after a period of 4 years. For banks and insurance companies, the threshold is based on one-tenth of total assets. A further criterion for Commission control is a threshold of Community-wide turnover of at least 250 million ECU for at least two of the companies concerned. In contrast, if each of the firms concerned derives two-thirds of their Community business in one and the same Member State, the merger will be subject to national control.

In contrast with the satisfaction experienced with a clear and definite agreement for the mergers' legislation, the compromise reached on the harmonisation of the rates and the principle for the value added tax (VAT) can only be described as disappointing. First, since the Member States would not accept the origin principle — mainly because they could not trust in the efficiency and fairness of a future central fund for redistributing tax revenues, we are left with the present destination principle. Furthermore, this system is likely to last for quite a long time. However, it was agreed that tax controls at frontiers will be removed early in 1993, differences between tax rates cannot be widened between now and then, and, that before the end of 1991, the final scheme concerning the normal rate and the list of products liable for the reduced rate and the scheme governing the zero rate will be defined.

It is, however, the acceptance of the banking directive which could have the most positive influence both inside the EEC as well as between the Community and third parties — particularly the United States. The main aim of this directive — apart from defining the solvency requirements for banks, was to create a European banking passport which would allow a bank, established in one EEC Member State, to set up business in the others. There then arose the question of reciprocity between the Community and third parties. The Commission was all for "hard" reciprocity which would have meant that sending countries would have been forced to grant EEC banks exactly the same rights as they enjoyed in the Community if their banks were to be granted the European banking passport. In the case of the United States, for example, it would have meant that EEC banks would have been granted national banking freedoms which American banks do not enjoy in their own country since U.S. banking is state and not national.

Fortunately, the "soft" option, as advocated by Lord Cockfield, was adopted. This means that so long as the sending countries give EEC banks the same rights as their own banks, then, their banks may qualify for the European banking passport.

If all goes well, the adoption of this directive could lead to a much-needed and healthy competition since Community citizens have access to a bigger choice of financial services. In the experience of the author, nowhere is this more necessary than in the Netherlands where the awful inefficiency and general unpleasantness of the banks are only equalled by the dreadfulness of the Dutch bureaucracy — both typical examples of "the unacceptable face of Calvinism".

The Community had already demonstrated its intention to (finally!) devote proportionately less of its resources to agriculture and more to social and regional policies in its decision to double spending in the latter areas between 1989 and 1993. This intention has been reinforced by the proposals for the common agricultural prices, made in February 1990, whereby those for North European products would be frozen whereas those for many Mediterranean ones would, in effect, be cut. Also, the policy of penalising over-production will be continued, and, may be, extended to other products. In contrast, the author discerns a movement to classify the plight of smaller poorer farmers as a social rather than an agricultural problem — and consequently to subsidise them directly (as is at present the case for hill farmers).

An area of particular controversy between Britain and the other EEC Members has been the Charter on Fundamental Social Rights. Correctly, Mrs. Thatcher estimated that a mandatory minimum Community wage would be "the kiss of death" for poorer regions and countries where wages are presently low because prospective richer North European and non-EEC investors would have little or no incentive to invest there. Wrongly, she assured that the demand for worker participation smacked of socialism. The strongest worker participation is, in effect, in West Germany.

In the event, clause 5 of the Charter, accepted by all Member States, except Britain, in December 1989, stated "all employment shall be fairly remunerated. To this effect, in accordance with arrangements applying in each country: workers shall be assured of an equitable wage, i.e. a wage sufficient to enable them to have a decent standard of living". Regarding, worker participation, the relevant clause (number 17) is equally modest. It states, "information, consultation and participation for workers, must be developed along appropriate lines, taking account of practices in force in the various Member States. This shall apply especially in companies or groups of companies having establishments or companies in several Member States of the European Community".

A policy area where little or no progress had been made, hitherto, but which is explicity laid down as an aim in the Treaty of Rome and which would have an important influence on regional and competition policies is transport policy. A common policy for transport is finally being developed. To date, a compromise on road haulage has been reached whereby more pan-European passes will be issued for a trial period with the proviso that no Member State should have more than 30 per cent of the total. Progress is also being made in the areas of sea and air transport.

In contrast, one notes little or no changes in energy policy. Perhaps this is because the policy objectives were already agreed upon some time ago and both the Commission and the Member States have sought to implement them.

The area of great on-going controversy is that regarding the moves towards an economic and monetary union. The furore has been caused by certain parts of the Delors Report, published early in 1989. Before entering into an analysis of these, apparently to some countries, provocative parts, the author finds it important to stress the following points.

An agreement to embark upon a full economic and monetary union was in fact reached by the Heads of State of the six Founder Members of the EEC at The Hague, at the end of 1969 — with the proviso, "provided the political will to do so exists". Furthermore, new Member States were "invited" to accept this decision. Then, following the publication and adoption of the second Werner Report, in October 1970, we have experienced the "Snake in the Tunnel", the "Snake Arrangement", and now, the European Monetary System. Thus, according to the author, we have been in the first stage of an EMU since April 1972 and the Delors Report simply repeats this fact. However, where this report seems to be breaking new ground and causing concern for the Deutsche Bundesbank, and, especially for Mrs. Thatcher, is that it has lead to proposals — strongly supported by France — for moves towards the second and third and final stages of an EMU and for a re-writing of the Treaty of Rome.

Turning more specifically to the Delors Report, there are certain clauses that require closer examination. Thus, clause 32 calls for the creation of a European System of Central Banks (ESCB), which, "acting through the Council — would be responsible for formulating and implementing monetary policy as well as managing the Community's exchange rate policy vis-à-vis third currencies". Clearly, this proposal implies the creation of an independent European Central Bank.

In the field of macro-economic policy (clause 33) the report calls for "effective upper limits on budget deficits of individual member countries" — as well as other limits on national economic sovereignty. It also calls for union by stages with the first one starting on 1st July 1990 — and with greater economic and monetary co-ordination from the outset. Even more important, it calls for a revision of the Treaty of Rome to accommodate all these proposals.

As already mentioned, the Germans are cautious about the later stages of union whilst Mrs. Thatcher is frankly hostile to them. The French are more than enthusiastic about the plan — the Italians almost equally so. In an attempt to show constructive criticism, the British have published the Major Report or Plan for a system of competing currencies (rather like the proposals made by Pascal Salin a decade ago) and the French have published the Guigou Report which lists the obstacles which will be encountered in implementing the Delors Report.

Despite the great controversy surrounding the publication of this report, it was agreed at the EEC Summit, in Madrid, in June 1989, that the first stage of the EMU (again!) would begin, as proposed by the report, on 1st July 1990. Then, in Strasbourg, in December of the same year, it was agreed that an inter-governmental conference would be held to examine the future stages of an EMU at the end of 1990.

So, what do all these policy changes and the events in Eastern Europe imply for the EEC and non-Member States in economic, political and social terms?

First, whatever the upheavals caused by the changes in Eastern Europe — and notably by the proposed monetary union between the two Germanies — the European Economic Community — at the centre of the extended European Economic Area, will, after 1992, emerge as the world's economic superpower. It will also have the potential to be the world's political superpower in international affairs. Here, the concern of non-Member States is, rightly, whether the EEC will become a "fortress Europe" or will opt for "open-ness"; we shall return to this option in the conclusions.

But, taking the policy changes, one by one, the author sees mixed results! The proposal to freeze, or, rather to reduce guaranteed agricultural prices is a return, finally, to economic sanity! At last, this scandalous misallocation of resources which has threatened to turn the EEC into a third world economic power instead of a highly sophisticated and technological union —

rivalling with Japan, for example — has been halted. At last we can put these resources to other uses. This is indeed progress. The banking directive is, equally, a plus for competition, and will, hopefully, lead to an increase in the welfare of citizens through the greater choice of services and financial instruments to which they will have access. In turn, costs for financial services should decline. In this sense, the adoption of the 'soft' reciprocity option is a positive sign. A word of warning, however, the present trend towards "bigness" in banking in Europe and the link-ups between banks in different countries does not bode well for competition. Only a strong presence by American and other banks will ensure an acceptable level of competition which will guarantee the well-being of citizens in the Community.

The author must express his disappointment at the paucity of progress achieved in the fiscal field. Whilst the compromise on VAT is better than nothing and despite the very workable proposals for excise duties put forward by the Commission, there has been absolutely no progress made with a Community Corporation Tax. Early in 1990, Madame Schrivener correctly sounded the alarm by stressing that we must have a common tax by 1993. She also pointed out that proposals for an EEC tax had been on the table for two decades. Equally, in a parallel field, the author is alarmed that we still do not have a European Company law — a legal instrument which will become a necessity for Community business by 1993.

At this point, reference should be made to the evolution in the Commission's proposals for a rapprochement between the principal excise duties. It will be noted that in the chapter by Walter Hahn, and in the Commission's proposals in August, 1987, very wide gaps existed in the different levels of national duties for the same products. Furthermore, the governments of some countries, notably Denmark and the Republic of Ireland — but, also, to some degree, the United Kingdom — rely very heavily on the

revenue from excise duties for their national budgets. Consequently, too great a degree of harmonization — downwards —
would be quite unacceptable for some countries. Thus, on 25th
October 1989, the Commission (though, not yet the Council)
agreed on a new set of proposals, as shown below. If accepted by
the Member States, the minimum rates or thresholds would come
into effect on 1st January, 1993. The target rates are not compulsory but indicate, rather, a desired orientation. Both sets of
rates would be re-examined every 2 years.

The effects of these tax changes, if accepted, have not yet been
costed. However, it is already clear that some countries will have

The Commission's Proposals for Excise Duties.

	Minimum rate	Target rate
Cigarettes: specific excise tax per 1,000	15 ECUs	21.5 ECUs
ad valorem + VAT	45%	54%
Other tobacco products (+ VAT)		
cigars, cigarillos, others	25%	36%
snuff	50%	56%
chewing tobacco	37%	43%
Alcoholic beverages		
alcohol for beverages (spirits) (hl)	1118.5 ECUs	1398.1 ECUs
wines (hl)	9.35 ECUs	18.7 ECUs
sparkling wines (hl)	16.5 ECUs	33 ECUs
beers (hl)	9.35 ECUs	18.7 ECUs
Petroleum products		
leaded petrol (1000 litres)	306 ECUs	340 ECUs
unleaded petrol (idem)	261 ECUs	295 ECUs
diesel (idem)	168—185 ECUs	177 ECUs
heating gas oil (idem)	47—53 ECUs	50 ECUs
heavy fuel oil (1000 kg)	16—18 ECUs	17 ECUs
LPG and methane (1000 litres)	77 ECUs	85 ECUs
lubricants	—	—

to make changes in their tax systems. Thus, for example, five countries — Greece, Italy, Portugal, Spain and West Germany — will have to create, for the first time, an excise duty on wine. In the case of diesel oil, many states will have to make adjustments.

Another area of the most considerable controversy in the field of fiscal integration concerns the Commission's proposals, made in February, 1989, for a Community-wide 15 per cent withholding tax on capital gains. As will be seen from the table below, some countries levy quite high withholding taxes, some do not impose them at all. In the case of the latter category, the most important exception is that of Luxembourg, which has threatened to use its right of veto to oppose the introduction of such a Community tax. Luxembourg is a tax haven, and regards the non-imposition of such a tax as a matter of national survival. Logically, in a common market, either one imposes the same Community-wide tax or none at all. Here, would it be possible, in the case of Luxembourg, to have a Dérogation or exemption?

Most recently, early this year, the Commission has started to examine national levels of social security taxes and personal income taxes. In a common market, which, at least officially, is not yet in a pre-federal stage, this would seem to be a very risky thing for the Commission to do. At this stage, the author does not know of one single Member State which would even begin to contemplate a harmonization of such taxes. Here, everyone would unite behind Mrs. Thatcher in the defence of their national sovereignty.

Having said this, it is clear that the demands of the Community budget will grow. Already, important increases have been agreed upon, until 1993, for social and regional spending. Now, there are the needs of our East European friends, which as a matter of basic European solidarity, must be met. Here, it is possible that the old idea of a Community energy tax will be resurrected. Failing this, a further increase in the ceiling of the national and weighted VAT as the basis for each Member State's contribution will have to be contemplated. The author shudders at the thought of the upheaval which such an eventuality will cause.

One final observation about the moves towards fiscal integration is necessary. Gradually, but surely, the room for manoeuvre of the Member States is becoming more restricted. In turn, their freedom to operate an economic demand policy is reduced. If and when, those parts of the Delors Report concerning restriction on budgetary deficits are accepted and as monetary union becomes stronger, then, the Member States will have abdicated most of their economic, fiscal and monetary sovereignty. Finally, the planned changes, for example, in excise duties, could lead to an increase or decrease in the consumption of the articles/products concerned — with all the related consequences for national and Community economic policies.

Withholding taxes — 1989.

Percent of interest income	On interest paid to	
	Residents	Non-residents
Belgium	25	25
Britain	25*	25*
Denmark	0	0
France	27—47	0—51
West Germany	10	10
Greece	8—25	49
Holland	0	0
Ireland	0—35	0—35
Italy	12.5—30	12.5—30
Luxembourg	0	0
Portugal	30	30
Spain	20	20

Source: Arthur Andersen   * Large deposits exempt

The moment the events in Eastern Europe started, existing trade agreements were upgraded and an offer of associated status — *not* leading to membership of the EEC — was proposed after the holding of free parliamentary elections in CMEA countries. But, in the immediate future, any increase in the present low levels of East-West trade will depend largely on the provision of Western credits and major changes in the economic, monetary and pricing structures of East European countries. Also, a major transfer of funds will be necessary.

Jacques Delors, President of the Commission, has suggested a minimum annual transfer from the EEC to Eastern Europe of 14 billion ECU's for five years. There will consequently be calls for an increase in the size of the Community budget. Equally, there will be enormous demands placed on the Federal German Republic to help the other Germany which will greatly increase budgetary problems for the EEC. In any case, as a consequence, for a few years, at least, the welfare of the Community's citizens is likely to remain stable or to decline. In the long run however Eastern Europe is likely to become an important market for Western products.

The agreement of mergers errs on the side of "bigness" — which does not augur well for competition. Here, the vigilance of the Commission will have to be sharpened.

Similarly, the author considers that the Commission, despite the temporary compromise reached in the field of road haulage, will have to be much more dynamic if we are to have a competitive transport policy by 1993. The savings which could be made in the fields of air transport and road haulage if a substantial degree of competition were introduced would be quite tremendous and the welfare benefits for consumers and producers alike would be very great. In contrast, a major victory for competition was the decision, by the Industry Ministers on 22nd

February, this year, to open up the Community's market for public purchasing to cross-border competition.

A compensation for workers is the Social Charter. This is a comprehensive and a noble document. It does lay down the minimum social standards to which any civilized democratic society should aspire. At the same time, it does, correctly, take account of national differences and preferences. The question which remains unanswered is, will it be applied to any great degree and will it lead to an increase in labor costs.

Finally, the proposal for a monetary union between the two Germanies with the DM as the unique currency is, to say the least, revolutionary. It will, whether the conversion between the two currencies is affected at a rate of 1 to 1 — or 1 to 2 or any other rate — have dramatic consequences for both Germanies, for the EEC and for the rest of the world. No ones welfare will remain unaffected.

Basically speaking, a conversion at the rate of 1 to 1 would unleash inflationary forces of such a magnitude inside West Germany which would destroy forty years of highly successful economic and monetary management. Indeed, during the course of the week ending 24th February, the five independent economic institutes and a number of banks in the Federal German Republic warned the Government of the dire consequences if such a conversion were applied. There was even talk of an "economic wasteland". Almost simultaneously there emerged proposals for a dual conversion rate. Thus, pensions and savings in the German Democratic Republic would be converted into DM's at a rate of 1 to 1. However, wages would be converted at a much lower rate, may be, for example, at a rate of 6 to 1. This latter rate would correspond, in some degree, to that adopted in the successful currency reform of 1948. It would, logically, have to be accompanied by the condition that a major proportion of the liquid assets would have to be frozen for some time.

Whichever combination is chosen, a number of consequences are already clear. The Federal German Republic will have at its disposal fewer resources to transfer to other Eastern European and to Third World countries. Some inflation will take place in West Germany. In order to counteract this tendency and to encourage an inflow of funds into the country, West German interest rates are almost bound to rise. There will then be a repercussion effect throughout the rest of Western Europe and elsewhere. There will be economic belt-tightening throughout the West. If the DM weakens, this could be good for the European Monetary System since it will make the other participating currencies more attractive and lead to a better balance in the system. If, in contrast, German interest rate rise too sharply, then currency re-alignments may be necessary.

Some observers believe that the proposed monetary union between the two Germanies could hasten the full economic and monetary union — though no reasons for such a conclusion are given. In contrast, the author thinks that the problems caused by this union could delay the second and third stages of an EMU. Logically, however, if, as is expected, the EEC becomes economically more integrated after 1992, then trade and business between the Member States could be facilitated by a move towards a full EMU. Such a move could also bring the Community closer to some form of political union (perhaps like the Swiss model?) — which will not be to everyone's taste.

CONCLUSIONS

The conclusions are indeed mixed. On the one hand, the expected increase in competition in some sectors should lead to a better allocation of resources and an increase in the welfare of citizens through a wider choice of goods and services and lower costs. On the other hand, the compromises reached and the lack of progress achieved elsewhere will tend to reduce efficiency and welfare. Also, a complete application of the Social Charter — whilst improving workers' rights — would, logically, tend to increase wage costs, and, consequently prices. Thus, the EEC would be less competitive internationally.

Events in Eastern Europe and the proposed monetary union between the two Germanies will necessitate a major transfer of economic resources from the EEC to our East European friends. Equally, there will be a propensity to inflation in the Community. In turn, the European Monetary System will become more necessary than ever before. Whether or not events in Eastern Europe will hasten or slow down moves towards a full EMU is open to discussion.

Thankfully, despite attempts by some countries, notably France and Italy, to stop imports of Japanese cars and electronic goods, and agreements, at least in principle, to demand quotas for European produced films and television programmes, the Community does not seem to have fallen for the temptation of creating "Fortress Europe". But, will we demand strict reciprocity in the field of public procurement? Here, the author hopes that the EEC will negotiate with friendly nations, notably the USA, and seek a general opening up of bidding, internationally, for public procurement. It should be noted that this important sector accounts for some 15 to 20 per cent of the Community's GDP — more than internal trade, in fact. However, ending on a note of optimism, the decision, reached on 22nd February, to which reference has already been made, to open up the Community's. Some 850 billion ECU market for public purchasing to cross-frontier competition, is indeed a major victory for competition, which, in turn, should lower costs, and, consequently increase the welfare of the Community's citizens.

Final Observations

The conclusions to this preface are clearly that these are indeed momentous times. Much, much has been agreed upon, and, despite the events in Eastern Europe, the moves towards the creation of a Single European Market by the end of 1992 are irrevocable. By the mid-1990's the Member States of the EEC will be more integrated, economically and probably, socially, than ever before and the desirability and feasibility of an EMU will become stronger. Then, if and when we do reach the final stage of an EMU, the demands for and need of a political union will become stronger and stronger. It is almost certainly this kind of inevitability to which Mrs. Thatcher is opposed.

Whatever happens, the Community, with its impending agreement for an even closer and deeper association with the countries of the EFTA, will have, by 1993, created a new European Economic Area or Space (EEA or S). More than ever before, it will be the economic and trading superpower of the world. The question which must still be asked is that despite the creation of a EEA or S and despite the special associate status which the Community is planning to offer East European countries — after the holding of free and fair parliamentary elections — will the EEC be ready to assume its political and monetary responsibilities at a world level? Until now, with a few exceptions in the field of foreign policy, it has shirked its responsibilities. Indeed, in the monetary field, apart from a brief national foray by De Gaulle in the 1960's, it has ignored them completely, but, the EEC will have to face these responsibilities. These, and other questions, will be examined in another work.

Amsterdam, Bonn and St. Paul, March 1990.

Acknowledgements

The editor wishes to thank Ben Kotmans of the Europa Instituut, University of Amsterdam, and Eva Weigold of the MIM Centre, University of St Thomas, St Paul, for their assistance in typing parts of this work.

Likewise, special thanks are due to my assistant, Patrick Dykhoff, for his help in preparing the index of this book.

Notes about the contributors

Peter Coffey, a British national, was, until recently, Head of the Economics section at the Europa Instituut, University of Amsterdam. Presently, he is holder of the recently created West Chair at the Graduate School at the University of St. Thomas, St. Paul, Minnesota, USA. He has published many works on European and international economic and monetary problems. Mr. Coffey, who speaks seven languages, has lectured in most countries of the EEC, as well as in many other parts of the world.

Elizabeth De Ghellinck, a Belgian national, is an assistant professor at the Centre de Recherches Interdisciplinaires Droit et Economie Industrielle (CRIDE) at the Catholic University of Louvain. She is also an associate professor of economics at the Catholic University of Mons, Belgium.

Walter Hahn, a German national, was, until recently, attached to the University of Saarbrücken. Now, he is working as a business economics analyst.

David Hawdon, a British national, is a Senior Lecturer in the Department of Economics at the University of Surrey, England. He has published many works on Energy Policy.

Willem Molle, a Dutch national, is Head of the Division Industrial and Location Studies at the Netherlands Economic Institute,

Rotterdam, and Professor at the University of Limburg in Maastricht. He has been for many years responsible for research on behalf of the EEC Regional Policy Directorate-General, and has published several works about regional and industrial questions.

Piet van den Noort, a Dutch national, is Professor of Agricultural Economics in the Department of Agricultural Economics at the Agricultural University of Wageningen. He has published many works about the EEC's Common Agricultural Policy.

The European Monetary System

PETER COFFEY

THE BACKGROUND

Like its predecessor, the "Snake" Arrangement,[1] the European Monetary System (EMS) was created largely (though by no means exclusively) as a manifestation of profound European concern at the irresponsibility of the U.S. Administration in the field of international monetary economics — notably the lack of any clear policy for the dollar. Also, like its predecessor, the EMS is an intermediary step on the road to a full economic and monetary union (EMU), as agreed upon by the Heads of Government of the original six founder Member States of the EEC in Den Haag at the end of 1969 — "provided that the political will to do so existed". This decision was a logical one since the countries — whose economies are open or very open ones (see Table 1) — were conducting half of their trade with each other, they had become highly integrated, the successful management of the Common Agricultural Policy (CAP) requires stable exchange rates, and, the Community — under the pressure of France — desired, as the world's most important trading bloc, to create its own "international monetary personality". The most logical way of achieving all these aims — as well as eventually creating a political union — was to create an EMU.

1

P. Coffey (ed.), Main Economic Policy Areas of the EEC — Toward 1992. pp. 1—27.
© *1990 Kluwer Academic Publishers, Dordrecht — Printed in the Netherlands.*

Table 1. EEC: Degree of "Open-ness" in National Economies in 1982 (as a percentage of GNP).

	Exports	Imports
Belgium	64.0	68.4
Denmark	36.8	36.3
France	22.2	24.0
Germany (West)	29.5	28.7
Greece	14.7	26.4
Ireland	53.2	68.1
Italy	24.7	28.2
Netherlands	58.9	54.9
United Kingdom	27.1	23.9
EEC Total	29.9	30.1

Source: EEC Commission, "European Economy", No. 12, July 1982.
Reproduced from P. Coffey, *The European Monetary System — Past, Present and Future*. Nijhoff, Dordrecht, 1984.

The practical manifestation of the "Snake" Arrangement was a narrowing of the band of fluctuation around the currencies of the participating countries to 2.25 per cent and this "Snake" did, for about one year, move inside the wider dollar tunnel of 4.5 per cent. However, as was demonstrated by the small number of countries remaining in the "Snake" at the end of its life in March 1979, the Arrangement lacked the most essential elements for success — the means of coordinating the economic and monetary policies of participating Member States together with the provision of adequate financial help for those countries facing balance-of-payments problems. Also, parity adjustments tended to be too late and too little in scope.

In contrast, the EMS is both more rigid and more flexible and contains a number of new features. In particular, at a more practical level, it does lay down quite clearly the steps to be undertaken by participating countries whenever their currencies come under pressure on the exchange markets.

THE BASIC ESSENTIALS OF THE SYSTEM

At the technical level, the EMS is similar to the "Snake" Arrangement. Thus, at the "GRID" or bi-lateral national currency to national currency level, the margin of fluctuation for a currency is still 2.25 per cent — with a special band of 6 per cent organised for the Italian Lira. However, this is not the rigorous part of the system. Instead, since the architects of the system intended that the ECU[2] should be the kingpin, the national currencies of the participating Member States fluctuate against the ECU within very narrow margins which have been "individualised" by the Commission (see Diagram 1 and Table 2). Apart from the extremely narrow maximum margins of fluctuation — the "maximum divergence spread", e.g. only 1.51 per cent in the case of West Germany, the participating countries are expected to start intervening when their currencies reach 75 per cent of this maximum band — the "Divergence Threshold". In the case of West Germany, for example, this is only 1.146 per cent.

It is therefore these "individualised" margins vis-à-vis the ECU which provide the real discipline and constraints to the system.

In contrast with its predecessor, the EMS, in the Resolution of the Council of Ministers of 5 December 1978, lays down quite clear step-by-step measures to be taken by a participating country wherever its currency comes under pressure. These are: — diversified intervention, — monetary measures, — drawing on credit facilities, and, — external and domestic policy measures.

The lack of credits under the old "Snake" System was one of its more serious defects. This important defect has been largely made

4

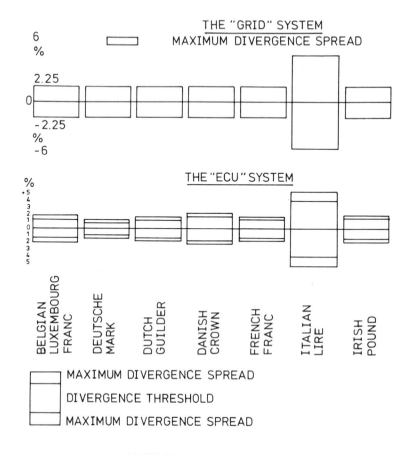

THE "GRID" SYSTEM
MAXIMUM DIVERGENCE SPREAD

THE "ECU" SYSTEM

BELGIAN LUXEMBOURG FRANC
DEUTSCHE MARK
DUTCH GUILDER
DANISH CROWN
FRENCH FRANC
ITALIAN LIRE
IRISH POUND

MAXIMUM DIVERGENCE SPREAD
DIVERGENCE THRESHOLD
MAXIMUM DIVERGENCE SPREAD

DIVERGENCE THRESHOLD
When a currency reaches the upper or
lower limits of this band, the Government concerned must intervene in the
exchange markets

Reproduced from: The European Monetary System — Six Months Later.
P. Coffey, Three Banks Review, December '79, London.

good under the EMS. Thus, the amount of credits available to
Member-States — should they face pressures on their currencies

Table 2. The Commission's "individualisation" of Maximum Divergence Spreads and Divergence Thresholds.

Currencies	Maximum Divergence Spread vis-à-vis the ECU	Divergence Threshold vis-à-vis the ECU (until 16. Sept. 1984)	Divergence Threshold after 16. Sept. 1984
	%	%	%
Belgian/Luxembourg Franc	2.03	1.52	1.543
Deutsche Mark	1.51	1.13	1.146
Dutch Guilder	2.01	1.51	1.516
Danish Crown	2.18	1.64	1.642
French Franc	1.80	1.35	1.366
Italian Lira	5.43	4.07	4.051
Irish Pound	2.22	1.67	1.667
Pound Sterling	—	—	—

and balance-of-payments problems — are substantially larger. In 1981, the approximate value of these credits was 25 billion units of account as compared with 11.45 billion units of account under the former system.

As already mentioned, it was intended that the ECU should be the centre-piece of the EMS. To this effect, the participating Member States — plus Greece and the United Kingdom — have exchanged 20 per cent of their official reserves of gold and U.S. Dollars for ECU's with the embryonic European Fund for Monetary Co-operation,[3] (EFMC). Furthermore, it was planned that, two years after the coming into operation of the system, i.e. in 1981, further "swaps"[4] of official reserves would be made for ECU's and that the afore-mentioned embryonic organ would become either a real and dynamic Fund or a kind of European Central Bank.

THE SYSTEM IN OPERATION

When the EMS came into operation in March 1979, the following countries became fully active members: Belgium, Denmark, France, Ireland, Italy, Luxembourg, the Netherlands and West Germany. Whilst not being active members of the system, Greece and the United Kingdom, did, at a later date, exchange 20 per cent of their reserves of gold and dollars for ECU's with the EFMC. In strong contrast with its predecessor, no participating Member State has left the EMS.

On the negative side, it must be said that the second stage of the EMS did not come into being in 1981, as was originally planned. Thus, in the face of strong opposition from the West German Bundesbank, no further swaps of official reserves were made for ECU's. In reality, since the official ECU's have been little used, there would seem to be little real need for more at the present time — the case of the commercial ECU being quite different. Also, no agreement was reached about the type of Fund or Central Bank which should be created — there being several different proposals on the table — which are examined later in this chapter.

Turning to one of the major aims of the EMS — monetary stability and a fall in the rates of inflation, the performance has, on the whole, been satisfactory. At first, inflation rates tended to rise and the levels to diverge, but, more recently, they have tended to fall, and, in some cases to converge (see Table 3).

Some countries, notably Belgium and France[5] — but also Italy — have undertaken strong measures to control inflation — using their membership of the EMS as a main argument vis-à-vis their nationals. Whenever, rates of inflation have diverged too sharply and too widely, pressures have built up on the inflating currencies in the exchange markets. Subsequently, parity adjustments have taken place within the system. In strong contrast with the "Snake"

Table 3. Consumer prices. Percentage changes from previous year.

	1980	1981	1982	1983	1984	1985	1986
Germany	5.5	6.3	5.3	3.3	2.4	2.2	−0.2
France	13.6	13.4	11.8	9.6	7.4	5.8	2.7
United Kingdom	18.0	11.9	8.6	4.6	5.0	6.1	3.4
Italy[a]	21.1	18.7	16.3	15.0	10.6	8.6	6.1
Belgium	6.6	7.6	8.7	7.7	6.3	4.9	1.3
Denmark	12.3	11.7	10.1	6.9	6.3	4.7	3.6
Greece	24.9	24.5	21.0	20.2	18.5	19.3	23.0
Ireland	18.2	20.4	17.1	10.5	8.6	5.4	3.8
Luxembourg[b,c]	6.3	8.1	9.4	8.7	4.6	4.1	0.3
Netherlands	6.5	6.7	6.0	2.8	3.3	2.3	0.2
Portugal[b]	16.6	20.0	22.4	25.5	29.3	19.3	11.7
Spain	15.5	14.6	14.4	12.2	11.3	8.8	8.8

[a] Index for households of wage and salary earners.
[b] Excluding rent.
[c] From 1985 new index.
Source: OECD.

Arrangement, under the EMS, these adjustments have, with two exceptions, been discreet and swift. In all cases, they have been appropriate since, the following day, all speculation ceased on the currency markets.

But, unexpectedly, pride of place in the EMS's record must go to the expansion in the case of the commercial ECU. At the official level this development has been surprising because it was not planned, and, indeed, there was no place for the private or commercial ECU in the agreement which set up the EMS. Rather, the expansion of the use of the ECU filled a need. For businessmen, engaged in international trade, and concerned about volatile exchange rates, the ECU is a model of stability because of its composition. In fact, it is a "risk spreader" and does represent the economic force of the EEC. Furthermore, at an international level, the rates of interest for ECU's have been particularly reasonable which has made them particularly interesting for businessmen in countries such as France and Italy.

As the US Dollar has come under suspicion, the commercial ECU has become attractive to countries outside the EEC — such as China, the USSR and Japan. Thus, the ECU is now among the top 5 currencies or units of account used for international commercial loans. Likewise, there has been an enormous increase in interbank assets and liabilities denominated in ECU's. In December, 1983, assets amounted to the equivalent of 6.9 billion dollars, and in December 1985, to 38.0 billion dollars. For the same periods, liabilities amounted to 7.0 and 34.3 billion dollars, respectively.

In most EEC Member States, citizens may either open a private bank account denominated in ECU's, or open bank accounts to receive credits and/or loans in ECU's. The principal country which did not give these rights its citizens was West Germany — this was fortunately changed on 17 June, 1987. However, there are signs that the Germans — and notably, the Bundesbank — are becoming less hostile in their attitude to the ECU.

Since June 1985, it has been possible to purchase travellers' cheques denominated in ECU's. Also, due to the great expansion in business, a clearing union for settling interbank accounts in commercial ECU's was set up at the B.I.S.

THE FUTURE OF THE EMS

The background

The future of the EMS will be deeply affected by the date 1992, when, a real common market in both goods and services will be created. The most important change relative to the EMS will be the complete freeing of capital movements between the Member

States, which, to the author, will, sooner or later, be accompanied by the adoption of a common policy towards borrowing on third party capital markets. In turn, this would seem to imply the adoption of joint policies towards such currencies as the Yen and the Dollar (as proposed by Mr. Balladur, the French Minister of Finance in an article in the Financial Times on 17 June, 1987) and common economic and monetary policies. In brief, as from 1992 onwards, the EEC would almost certainly move on to a much more integrated form of union, in reality, an economic and monetary union. All this, would apart from the adoption of the afore-mentioned common policies, necessitate the creation of at least one common monetary organ.

It is therefore advisable to examine these imminent changes and to make relevant proposals well in advance of 1992. To the author, there are principal areas to which Governments, Community officials, bankers and academics should already be turning their attention. These areas, which are by no means definitive, are:

i) the removal of obstacles to the freeing of capital and monetary movements;
ii) the removal of obstacles to the establishment of financial services between Member States;
iii) the co-ordination of economic and monetary policies;
iv) the future use of the official ECU;
v) the future use of the commercial ECU;
vi) the creation of an 'active' European Monetary Organ (EMO);
vii) possible future new 'active' members of the EMS; and
viii) the adoption of common economic and monetary policies towards third parties.

As already stated, this list of areas is by no means exhaustive — but, to the author, it does contain the essential questions which should be tackled without further delay. Agreements have now been made concerning i) and several areas of ii).

(i) *The removal of obstacles to the freeing of capital movements*

To the author, there are two distinctly contradictory types of obstacles which militate against the freeing of capital movements. The first type is basically a national capital market, government and/or national banking system giving priority in borrowing to their own nationals (whether individuals or institutions) over nationals of other Member States. This preference is clearly an infringement of the Treaty of Rome. However, when the author conducted research in this area, in 1984,[6] he observed the following state of affairs among the nine countries examined, Belgium, Britain, Denmark, France, Germany, Ireland, Italy, the Netherlands and Luxembourg All the nine countries intervened officially in the bond market. Six countries openly intervened to stabilise short-term bond prices, whilst two others intervened moderately. Five countries intervened to influence the slope and position of the yield curve and two intervened moderately. In three cases, outright priority in borrowing was given to the domestic public sector whilst five other countries pursued the same policy in a moderate manner. Only one country gave outright priority to domestic borrowers — in the other eight cases, the situation was nebulous.

The other type of obstacle is a straight control by government over movements of money and capital by their nationals from their countries to other Member States and/or controls over borrowing by their nationals in other EEC countries. Here, more recently, the major culprits have been France, Italy, Greece and the Republic of Ireland. Most recently, the first two countries have been relaxing currency controls.

It is clear that both these groups of preferences and controls will have to disappear from 1992 onwards. There is another area where changes will have to be made — this is the question of budgetary deficits. This question, however, will be examined in the chapter dealing with the co-ordination of economic and monetary policies.

(ii) *The removal of obstacles to the establishment of financial services between member states:*

The freeing of the establishment of services is a basic cornerstone of a common market, and, as such, is one of the principal aims of the Treaty of Rome. Until most recently, little, if anything, had been achieved in this field.

Indeed, in the 1983 Communication[7] on Financial Integration sent by the Commission to the Council, the conclusion was reached that "the freeing of the intra-Community capital movements is now less free than it was in the 1960's". To the author, practically no progress has been made since the publication of the Segré Report in 1966.[8]

Fortunately, more recently, under the joint pressure of the Netherlands and the United Kingdom, the following proposals and progress have been observed:

In October, 1985, the Commission of the European Communities made a number of proposals for the strengthening of the European Monetary System.

These proposals concerned the inclusion of the System in the Treaty of Rome, the transformation of the present somewhat embryonic European Fund for Monetary Co-operation (hereafter referred to as the EFMC) into a "real" Fund which might become a form of European Central Bank, and a call for Greece and the United Kingdom to become "active" members of the EMS.

The Commission's proposals almost coincided with decisions taken by the Council of Ministers to enable unit trusts based in any one EEC Member State to sell to investors in other Common Market countries (with some reservations expressed by Denmark).

The two directives concerning this decision will become effective in 1989. Also, the Ministers agreed to allow an exchange of ECU's between Community organs and central banks with equivalent third party institutions.

More recently, on 22 May, 1986, Mr. Jacques Delors, the President of the European Commission, announced details of a two phase plan to liberalise all remaining exchange controls on capital movements by 1992. The first phase, which took the form of a draft directive to the Council of Ministers, the following month, formally proposed the scrapping of exchange controls in the Community for dealings in unlisted stocks and shares, floating of new share issues on stock exchanges and long-term trade credits. Such liberalisation moves would be mandatory and not voluntary as at the present time.

In the second place, all monetary and financial flows in the Community would be liberalised. Thus, EEC nationals would be able to have bank accounts in any Community currency, to save or borrow, or take out a mortgage across national boundaries. Similarly no restrictions on the use of credit cards and Euro-cheques would exist.

(iii) *The co-ordination of economic and monetary policies*

It is clear that the feasibility of an economic and monetary union will depend on the degree of success achieved by the members in co-ordinating their economic and monetary policies. It was precisely the lack of co-ordination between participants that led to the downfall of the old Snake Arrangement. In comparison, the EMS has, to date, been more successful than its predecessor.

This is a critical area for the future of the EMS because many variables and considerations conflict with each other. Basically, the EMS is a transitional phase (a de-facto monetary union) somewhere between the old Snake Arrangement and a full economic and monetary union. This implies that whilst, on the one hand, Member States are concerned about annual (or even quarterly or monthly) balance-of-payments questions among themselves and between them and third parties, they must also be aware of comparative rates of inflation. In both cases, measures may be taken (for example increases in interest rates) which militate against an eventual freeing of capital movements and therefore the achievement of a full EMU. Furthermore, when a full EMU is achieved, Member States loose the right to vary the parity of their currencies between themselves, and, inter-Community balance-of-payment deficits are then replaced by intensified regional imbalances. This implies that the EEC will have to adopt an active regional policy in advance of the achievement of a full EMU. To date, there are no signs of this happening.

In one crucial area, the 'active' participants in the EMS have achieved much since they, like all West European countries, have adopted as their public economic policy goal the control of inflation. They have also made progress in reducing the levels of inflation — in some cases inflation rates are converging. Unfortunately, in the case of some Member States, this has been achieved partly through high interest rates and exchange controls.

Another area where action will have to be taken both before and after 1992 is that of public sector deficits. Apart from the inflationary potential inherent in important and persistant deficits, this can also lead to a "crowding out" effect in capital markets which could not be tolerated in a fully integrated European Capital Market.

In an article in 1986,[9] John Bispham drew attention to this problem and recognized that only a few EEC countries were using discipline with their public debt. A further problem observed by the author in his own research is that of the length of maturity of the public debt as well as the amount. This is a question which would have to be resolved after 1992.

(iv) and (v) *The future use of the official and commercial ECU*

To the author, if the ECU is to fulfill the role of both a reserve asset and a currency, it should play the following rôles:

i)   a unit of account;
ii) a medium of exchange (between individuals);
iii) a means of settlement (between institutes, central banks, governments and similar bodies);
iv) a store of value, and,
v)   a refuge from economic and/or political instability. In this last case, individuals and/or institutes may be willing to forego (at least partially and/or temporarily) the attractiveness of the currency or asset as a store of value; in exchange for enhanced security.

A number of observers seem to be confused by the existence of both official and commercial ECU's. Part of the confusion stems from the fact that the official ECU's have hardly ever been used (although all the official financial transactions of the Community are expressed in ECU's) and rates of interest for the two units have differed. More recently, however, the interest rates have tended to converge. Thus, the differences between the two kinds of ECU have become more blurred.

At the time of writing, the ECU plays the following roles:

i)   it is the unit of account for all official transactions of the EEC;
ii) it is a form of medium of exchange between individuals in that Community nationals may purchase travellers' cheques denominated in ECU's. In many countries (also in West Germany as from 17 June 1987), citizens may open up ECU-denominated bank accounts. Also, an increasing number of companies are quoting their contracts in ECU's;
iii) The ECU can be used as a means of settlement between Community Institutions, Governments and Central Banks of

the EEC. Furthermore, the Council of Ministers has agreed that exchanges of ECU's may be made with official organisations outside the Community — such as, for example, the International Monetary Fund.

iv) the ECU is not only an eminent store of value but it is remarkably stable. According to a Federal Trust study[10] the ECU has been the most stable of all currency units. This stability is inherent in its composition which gives it the most attractive additional quality as a "risk spreader". It is not, however, an attractive objective of speculation.

v) In view of its great stability and the fact that it represents the economic and financial weight of the Community, the ECU is an attractive refuge from economic and political instability.

Apart from fulfilling all these roles, the ECU is one of the two most important reserve assets in the world, and, is always among the top five currency units used in floating international commercial loans. Also, it should be noted that many, many countries outside the EEC — including Japan, China and the Soviet Union — have bought ECU's and/or taken up ECU-denominated loans.

Despite the progress made in a very short period of time, much greater progress in the use of the ECU would have to be made before and after 1992. Inside the Community, it would be normal to expect all EEC citizens to be given the right to open ECU-denominated bank accounts. Also, as the CEPREM Working Party on the Future of the ECU and the EMS proposed in 1987, ECU's should be used for intra-Community trade.

The author has, for many years, now suggested that a part of international trade in commodities should be denominated in ECU's. This is particularly desirable since it is the Community — and not the United States — which is the most important world trader in commodities. Further, in specific cases, such as that of Brazil, where the EEC is that country's major trading partner it would be logical for a portion of that trade to be conducted using

ECU's. One would envisage a future international economic order when world trade would be conducted using ECU's, Yens, Dollars, and, hopefully, convertible roubles.

Looking to the more immediate future, after 1992 with the removal of all internal obstacles to the free movement of goods and capital and the establishment of financial and other services, a more optimal allocation of resources will be possible — accompanied by a greater degree of efficiency. Thus, the Community will become more integrated and the arguments for a greater internal use of the ECU will be stronger. The greater use of the ECU will increase the need for creating a real active European Monetary Institution — it is to the different plans for such an institution to which we shall now turn. Before doing so, it should be stressed that the official ECU is still an official unit of account whereas the commercial ECU has been created to fulfill a genuine commercial need. Although, at the outset, the different rates of interest for the two ECU's caused some confusion among observers, the convergence of the two rates means that differences between the two tend to disappear.

The creation of an 'active' monetary organ

Before launching into a discussion about the rival merits of different kinds of monetary organisations, it is useful to examine the present situation regarding the responsibilities for managing the EMS. These are as follows:
a) the overall responsibility for the daily management of the EMS lies with the Commission, which, on a daily basis, calculates the value of the ECU against the national currencies of the individual EEC Member States as well as against important third party currencies such as the U.S. Dollar.
b) Decisions about changes in the structure and policies of the EMS, such as new 'swaps' of official ECU's, are taken by the Council of Ministers.

c) Intervention, each day, on the currency markets, both at the Grid and the ECU levels, is undertaken by the central banks of the individual Member States.

d) Although, 'legally speaking' the 'swaps' of ECU's and credits are made with the embryonic EFMC, in reality, they are made with B.I.S.

e) Similarly, it is the B.I.S. which acts as a clearing union for the commercial ECU's. It also manages the Community's short- and medium term credits.

Clearly, this situation is not satisfactory, and, as the commercial ECU is more widely used and as the Common Market becomes more integrated, then the need to create a more active kind of institution wherein most responsibilities could be grouped will become more pressing.

There are, it is true, many proposals on the table for the creation of such a monetary organ. A masterly choice is presented in the European Economy, nos. 7 and 12, for example. The Ceprem Working Party, based in Lyon, but normally meeting in Brussels, is working on new proposals, and, M. Louis, of the Belgian Central Bank, is in the process of elaborating a constitution for a European Central Bank. Then, in general discussions about this matter, at one extreme, the British give the impression that they would be happy to see the creation of a kind of regional IMF whilst the Bundesbank, at the other extreme, insists that West Germany could only accept a fully independent European Central Bank.

To the author, many of these discussions appear to be somewhat unrealistic because, basically, we should consider two time scenarios. One is post 1992, when, it is assumed, that a great deal of integration will take place; the other scenario is between now and then.

Clearly, if, as we expect, the Community does have a real common market with widespread use of the ECU, then, it would be necessary to create some form of Federal Reserve Board —

probably using the existing national control banks as branches. The degree of independence enjoyed by such an organ could be decided upon at its creation, but, it would at the very least be endowed with the following responsibilities:

i) the creation of ECU's — this could be done against national currencies and/or official reserves.

ii) The management of monetary policy through open market operations (O.M.O.), reserve requirements, and, interest rates.·

iii) The defence of the ECU in international money markets.

iv) The giving of advice to the Council of Ministers about economic and monetary policy.

These would, then, be the minimum responsibilities of a future central bank, and, certainly this organ would be endowed with other responsibilities. In the meantime, however, the author considers that this is the best moment to give life to the present embryonic EFMC. The following responsibilities should immediately be transferred to this 'real' European Monetary Fund:

i) the "lender of last resort" as the clearing union for commercial ECU's. Here, the Fund should be able to extend lines of credit in ECU's to commercial banks.

ii) The management of the short — and medium-term credits in the framework of the EMS.

iii) The management of the three-monthly central bank 'revolving' swaps against ECU's.

Also the Fund should be empowered to:

iv) organise swaps of ECU's against national currencies of the Community Member States.

v) organise swaps of ECU's against dollars with the Federal Reserve Board, and

vi) organise emergency supplies of ECU's, EEC national currencies and dollars for EEC Member States facing temporary and sudden shortages of such currencies.

Finally:

viii) The Fund would be responsible for the future creation of any new issues of ECU's.

The taking of these non-revolutionary decisions by the Council of Ministers would not require any national constitutional changes and would not (as seems to be the fear of a number of central banks) lead to the creation — in even the medium-term — of a European Central Bank. However, these decisions should be taken quickly since there is a danger of a kind of ECU anarchy arising within the Common Market if they are not taken.

(vi) *Future 'active' members of the EMS*

The background

Greece, Portugal and the United Kingdom are not 'active' members of the EMS — members engaged in the exchange-rate mechanism (ERM). However, as has already been mentioned, Greece and Britain are 'non-active' members.

At the outset, it should be stressed that if these four countries should wish to join the ERM, then not only would they have to subscribe to a public economic policy goal of controlling inflation, but their inflation rates would have to be fairly low. Furthermore, Portugal and Spain could not seriously envisage the possibility of becoming 'active' members until the end of their transitional period as members of the EEC at which time their national currencies will become an integral part of the ECU.

To date, only Spain has become a full member of the system. To back up this statement of intent, Spanish rates of inflation have been falling to levels which are really quite low but Spanish interest rates are very high.

In contrast, neither Greece nor Portugal have expressed any

intention of joining the EMS and their inflation rates remain relatively high.

The most animated interest and discussion revolves around the desirability — or otherwise — of Britain joining the EMS. Both the Commission and the Bundesbank have been making increasingly persistent calls for the United Kingdom to join. More recently, strong calls have been made by the Confederation of British Industry (CBI) in their desire for a stable Pound Sterling.

There have been many, many articles putting forward the case for and against British membership. Most recently, an exhaustive article in, The Economist,[11] did not come to any definitive conclusion. But, other contributions have been more categorical in their warnings and/or conclusions. Thus, for example, two articles in the Financial Times, written by the very dissimilar Samuel Brittan[12] and Bryan Gould,[13] urge extreme caution before taking such a step. In fact, the latter writer, like the Labour Party which he represents, is formally opposed to British membership.

Situated somewhat more in the middle of the discussion, the House of Lords Select Committee on the European Communities[14] does give the impression that British room for manoeuvre in the field of economic policy would be circumscribed as a member of the System.

In contrast, both the London Business School[15] and the Federal Trust[16] believe that membership would lead to a greater deal of exchange rate stability. The former report considers that inflation would be lowered if the exchange rate of the Pound Sterling were linked to that of the Deutsche Mark.

All these arguments lead one to ask the basic question, what are British economic and monetary policy aims and would membership of the EMS help Britain to achieve them? As has already been observed in the original text of this work, all West European countries, including Britain, have, for the first time in decades, opted for the same public economic policy goal, i.e. the control of inflation. In the case of some countries — notably France and Belgium — the national authorities believe that membership of the EMS does help them to control inflation because if they do not reduce levels of inflation then unacceptable pressures will build up on their currencies.

In the particular case of Britain, a number of somewhat more complex factors have to be taken into consideration. First, the Pound Sterling is a petro-currency, and consequently tends to display a greater degree of volatility than other European currencies. This would seem to imply that should Britain join the EMS, then, on occasions, the Bank of England may have to intervene massively in the exchange markets in order to maintain the agreed parity of currency. Also, wide variations in interest rates may be necessary. Both of these factors contain inflationary implications which may also cause unwelcome tensions within the System.

At a fundamental technical level, the question must be asked, what weapons do the British Authorities wish to use in the management of the national economy? During the first years of the Thatcher Administration, much publicity was given to the use of the control of the monetary supply as the main weapon. More recently, one gains the impression, that, having used different definitions for money supply, this weapon is no longer fashionable. Thus, perhaps, greater emphasis should be placed (as is done in West Germany) on the use of exchange rate policy as the principle economic and monetary tool. Here, however, it is essential that Britain try to choose a suitable exchange rate for Sterling particularly vis-à-vis the Deutsche Mark — if she is going to rely on this tool for the management of national economic policy.

The author's view

The author was recently asked by a British Member of the European Parliament what sort of advice he would give Mrs.

Thatcher about British membership of the EMS. The author replied that he would switch the question round and ask the Prime Minister two specific questions:

i) what are Britain's economic and monetary aims?
ii) would British membership of the EMS help the United Kingdom to achieve these aims?

Should the answer to the first question be monetary stability, the control of inflation and a fairly stable value for the Pound Sterling, then, the author would advise the British Government to take the currency into the ERM. In so doing, he would stress three points:

i) a 'realistic' value of the Pound Sterling must be established — particularly vis-à-vis the Deutsche Mark.
ii) Britain would have to consider the possibility of establishing a wider margin of fluctuation for the British currency than that existing for most other currencies. To the author it should be somewhere between the 2.25 per cent for the majority and the 6.00 per cent margin formerly for Italy and now, for Spain.
iii) It is essential that Britain establish that she either possesses adequate reserves or can call upon credits in order to intervene in the exchange markets whenever this may be necessary.

CONCLUSIONS — THE FUTURE — WHAT MIGHT HAPPEN — WHAT SHOULD HAPPEN

It is obvious that the Community finds itself on the threshold of the most important changes and developments since the beginning of the EEC. Alone, the freeing of capital movements will make changes inside the EMS inevitable. Similarly, an increased use of the commercial ECU will place such pressures on the role of the B.I.S. as a clearing union that the Community will be forced, finally, to create an 'active' European Monetary Fund.

However, in advance of the inevitability of change being forced on the Community, the Council, the Commission and the Parliament should, together, initiate a few fundamental and desirable changes. To the author, there are at least three important moves which should be undertaken; these are:

 i) by the end of the transitional phase leading to full Portuguese and Spanish membership of the EEC, all Community Nationals should have the right to open ECU-denominated bank accounts.

ii) The Community should actively encourage the use of the ECU in international trade. This should be introduced for intra-EEC trade as well as for trade with third parties where the Community is the main or one of the principal trading partners. This should certainly be done in the field of commodities where the EEC is the most important trading partner in the world.

iii) The EEC should immediately transform the present embryonic EFMC into a real 'active' European Monetary Fund endowed with all the functions described earlier in this chapter. Most especially, this Fund — or until its creation, the B.I.S. — should be empowered to grant lines of credit in ECU's to commercial banks. This last point is a matter of most urgent necessity.

As the author has proclaimed for many years, "the European Monetary System is foredoomed to be a success". However, it is preferable to achieve this in an orderly and thoughtful manner — rather than under the pressure of imminent chaos.

POSTSCRIPTUM

Since the completion of this chapter, a number of important moves and proposals have been made to strengthen the EMS.

The most important action concerns the removal of exchange

restrictions and the freeing of capital movements. On the 1st January, this year, France, after controlling capital and monetary movements for over 40 years, removed all exchange controls. Contrary to the expections of some analysts, no speculative outflows of capital from France occurred. Then, as had already been agreed in the framework of the SEM, by 1st July, eight Member States had removed controls over capital movements. Of the other countries, Spain and Ireland have agreed to free capital movements by the end of 1992, whilst Greece and Portugal may, in principle, keep theirs until 1995.

In the area of financial services, a directive aimed at opening up the EEC's highly protected and lucrative non-life insurance market was proposed by Sir Leon Brittan on 18th July. If accepted, it would give citizens a greater choice of premiums, and, through increased competition, cut costs. In principle, the directive will allow any insurance company established inside the EEC to offer all types of insurance, other than life insurance, in other Member States and to set up branches based on "home" country control. As in the case of banking an insurance passport is planned. This raises the question of reciprocity vis-à-vis third party countries and whether 'hard' or 'soft' reciprocity is envisaged. On the outcome of this question will depend the degree of competition in the insurance industry and consequently the welfare of consumers.

Finally, the debate about the future of the EMS and the ECU continues unabated. In June, Mr. John Major, the British Chancellor of the Exchequer, put forward a plan for the introduction of a "hard ecu" (to be used as a parallel currency) and the creation of a European Monetary Fund. A month later, Mr. Karl Otto Pöhl, President of the West German Bundesbank, courteously but firmly, rejected these proposals — pointing out that the EMS had gone beyond the stage of parallel and competing currencies. All these plans and counter-proposals do not seem to tackle the question as to whether Member States are fully aware of the consequences implied by a transfer of economic, monetary and political sovereignty to central organs (and an accompanying co-ordination of policies) which a full EMU entails.

Hopefully, these implications will be examined, in depth, at the intergovernmental conference on the next stages in the moves towards an EMU, to be held in Rome, in December, this year.

NOTES

1. A more detailed account of the background to and the workings of the "Snake" Arrangement may be found in P. Coffey, *The European Monetary System — Past, Present and Future*, Second Edition, Nijhoff, Dordrecht, 1986.
2. The ECU (European Currency Unit) was recalculated on 16 September, 1984, (coming into effect on the following day) to give the following composition:

The New Composition: as a percentage of the Total.		The New Composition of the ECU in National Currencies.
Deutsche Mark	32	0.719
French Franc	19	1.31
Pound Sterling	15	0.0878
Italian Lira	10.2	140
Dutch Guilder	10.1	0.256
Belgian Franc	8.2	3.71
Danish Kronor	2.7	0.219
Greek Drachma	1.3	1.15
Irish Punt	1.2	0.00871
Lux. Franc	0.3	0.16

The redefinition of the ECU was made by using the following formula:

$$P_i = \frac{Q_i}{C_i}$$

Where: P_i = weight of currency; Q_i = fixed quantity of currency; C_i = ECU exchange rate of currency: per ECU.

3. At a legal level, the agreement creating the Fund was made in April 1973. However, since it was not possible to reach agreement on the site of the Fund (the contestants being London and Luxembourg) most of the activities which it should execute are in fact done by the Bank for International Settlements (B.I.S.) in Basel, Switzerland.

4. This arrangement, a 3-monthly "revolving swap", was made in order to enable the ownership of the reserves to remain with the Member States.

5. It is worth noting that the French government did ask the question in 1983, of staying in or of leaving the IMF. They decided to remain in the system.

6. See the author's *The European Monetary System — Past, Present and Future*, op cit.

7. Communication from the Commission to the Council, COM (83) 274 final — Brussels, 24 May 1983.

8. EEC Commission, "The Development of a European Capital Market", Brussels, 1966.

9. Bispham, John, "Growing Public Sector Debt: a Policy Dilemma". *National Westminster Bank Quarterly Review*, London, May 1986.

10. Federal Trust, "The Time is Ripe", London, November 1984.

11. "European Monetary System. Why Sterling should join". *The Economist*, London, 4 July, 1987.

12. Samuel Brittan, "Fallacies on EMS Entry", *Financial Times*, 1 April 1986.

13. Bryan Gould, "Why Britain must resist the lure of the EMS", *Financial Times*, 7 May, 1986.

14. House of Lords Select Committee on the European Communities, "European Monetary System", First Report, HMSO, London, 1983.

15. *The London Business School, Economic Outlook*, vol. 9, no. 10, November, 1985, Gower Publishing House, England.

16. Federal Trust, "The Time is Ripe", London, November, 1984.

APPENDIX I: THE EUROPEAN MONETARY SYSTEM: RECORD

1979: March 13   Introduction of the EMS.
       September 23   Adjustments within the EMS.
                        1) a 5% re-evaluation of the Deutsche Mark vis-à-vis
                           the Danish Crown,
                        2) a 2% re-evaluation of the Deutsche Mark vis-à-vis
                           the Belgian, French and Luxembourg Francs, the
                           Dutch Guilder, the Italian Lira and the Irish Pound.

1980:	November 27	A 5% devaluation of the Danish Crown within the EMS.
1981:	March 23	A 6% devaluation of the Italian Lira within the EMS.
	October 4	A $5\frac{1}{2}$% revaluation of the Deutsche Mark and the Dutch Guilder.
		A $3\frac{1}{2}$% devaluation of the French Franc and the Italian Lira within the EMS.
1982:	February 21	A $8\frac{1}{2}$% devaluation of the Belgian Franc.
		A 3% devaluation of the Danish Crown within the EMS.
	June 12	A 4.25% revaluation of the Deutsche Mark and the Dutch Guilder.
		A 5.75% devaluation of the French Franc.
		A 2.75% devaluation of the Italian Lira — all within the EMS.
1983:	March 21	A 5.5% revaluation of the Deutsche Mark.
		A 3.5% revaluation of the Dutch Guilder.
		A 2.5% revaluation of the Danish Krone.
		A 1.5% revaluation of the Belg/Lux. Franc.
		A 2.5% devaluation of the French Franc and the Italian Lira.
		A 3.5% devaluation of the Irish Pound.
1985:	July 21	A 6% devaluation of the Italian Lira.
		A 2% revaluation of the Deutsche Mark, the Dutch Guilder, the Danish Krone, the Belg/Lux. Franc, the French Franc and the Irish Pound.
1986:	April 7	A 3% revaluation of the Deutsche Mark, and the Dutch Guilder.
		A 1% revaluation of the Belg/Lux. Franc and the Danish Krone.
		A 3% devaluation of the France Franc.
	August 2	A 8% devaluation of the Irish Pound.
1987:	January 11	A 3% revaluation of the Deutsche Mark and the Dutch Guilder.
		A 2% revaluation of the Belgian and Luxembourg Francs.
1989:	June 19	Spain joins Exchange Rate Mechanism of the EMS with a margin of fluctuation of 6%.
	September 21	ECU composition redefined to include Spanish Peseta and Portuguese Escudo.
1990:	January	A 3% devaluation of the Italian Lira. A narrowing of the margin of fluctuation for the Italian Lira to 2.25%.

The contribution of agriculture protection to European integration

PIET VAN DEN NOORT

WHY AGRICULTURAL PROTECTION IN THE EEC?

The Common Agricultural Policy is a price policy, giving farmers a price-guarantee and protection from outside suppliers. Why is that? It is a fact that all capitalist countries have agricultural protection in one form or another and for various reasons. One of the best reasons is the free market's inability to reach stability and to achieve income parity for farmers. There are also other reasons. Switzerland and Sweden have protected their agriculture so that in times of war, in which they prefer to be neutral, their agriculture and food supply can be independent. Also, the conservation of agricultural topsoil and landscape can be a reason for agricultural protection; for example as in Norway of Austria. There are countries with a long tradition of agricultural protection, such as France and Germany, but most other countries have only had such policies since the great depression of the 1930s.

Now, we could say that just as each individual country has protection for its agriculture, so the EEC has such a policy for itself. This seems to be a logical explanation, but it does not explain all problems. Why is there no common policy in other fields where each country traditionally had its own far-reaching policy measures? Why is agriculture a lone forerunner in the field

29

P. Coffey (ed.), Main Economic Policy Areas of the EEC — Toward 1992. pp. 29—52.
© *1990 Kluwer Academic Publishers, Dordrecht — Printed in the Netherlands.*

of common policies? Given the ideal of unity underlying the EEC we might have expected common social, fiscal and monetary policies and also common policies in the fields of research, energy, environment or transport. Other cases of economic integration (Benelux, EFTA, LAFTA, CACM, ACM) have no common agricultural policies.[10]

So there must be an additional factor. It is useful to remind us that economic integration was a third attempt to reach political integration in Europe; that is, to agree on a policy for achieving a stable, democratic order in Europe, with reconciliation between France and Germany, no wars or revolutions, but peace and security. The earlier attempts at unification were the Marshall Plan, and the European Coal and Steel Community. The third attempt should have been the European Defence Community but this treaty was not ratified by the French National Assembly in 1954.

Integrating the economics in Europe, however, was also a means for achieving more stability and peace. Germany was all in favour of this policy, not least because it has much to gain from a large industrial market. Unlike Germany, France believed that its comparative economic strength was in agriculture production. Post-war France could therefore only agree to join the integration policies provided it could expand its markets for agricultural products in Europe, in exchange as it were, for German industrial expansion. The participation of France was essential: its government was prepared to play it hard, (it has already refused to ratify the E.D.C. Treaty) so the other countries involved thought it wise to humour France. This "grain deal" would give France access to the European agricultural markets, Germany could expand its industrial markets, and political integration could proceed. The deal had, of course, its "conditions". The U.S. as a traditional grain supplier agreed to retreat a little for the greater good of political integration, but was unwilling to relinquish a considerable part of the European Market. The consumers and taxpayers implicitly agreed to use more French grain provided the policy did not become too expensive i.e. prices did not become too high. Farmers in Germany, on the other hand, were willing to co-operate, providing their losses were made good. It is therefore not surprising to find these provisos in the form of "goals" in the Treaty of Rome; in principle the deal was simple, but its imple-mention was only achieved by much hard work on the part of the politicians.

It is clear that France wanted to expand its agricultural pro-duction throughout the Euro-market and therefore demanded a market policy for agricultural and not an income-deficiency pay-ment system or social measures for farmers. To have a market means nothing without price guarantees, so the second aim of the common policy proposed for the EEC was a price policy. The aim was for the price of French wheat to a least meet the level of production costs in France, as otherwise a Common Market would not be no interesting proposition for the French. The EEC Member States were to give preference to French wheat: this was done by creating an artificial price difference with the world market by means of imposing a levy on imported grain ("com-munity preference").

It was difficult to arrive at a common acceptable price level and therefore at a common tariff or levy on grain. The French national price level was not acceptable to the Germans and the German level was not acceptable to the other Member States or to tradi-tional overseas suppliers. So the conclusion was that the common price level should be somewhere in between and should be found during a transitional period of some twelve years!

Within the EEC, France directed its political attention to securing a watertight guarantee of the grain deal by attempting to secure detailed regulations for agricultural markets. Outside the EEC trade policy was paramount for France: for example during the Kennedy Round, when the EEC (and also the individual Member States) negotiated about tariffs, mainly on industrial goods. France, however, was not prepared to accept an attractive deal in this area unless there was also an agreement about the tariffs on agricultural products (and in fact also about the common price in the EEC). The stand taken by France was extremely effective and the EEC countries also agreed on the common price of wheat (106 "Units of Account" per ton). This, combined with the detailed market regulations, gave an almost complete common agricultural price policy (see Table 1). It was set up as a system of protection with in fact unlimited guarantees. The most important flaw was that no agreement had been reached over the wheat price in years to come. Politicians played on this weak spot during prolonged negotiations (marathon sessions). No wonder France was in favour of an automatic procedure, a so-called "objective method", for fixing future prices. Although such a method was adopted, it never became a really automatic procedure!

Thus, the common agricultural price policy was necessary to obtain French co-operation, without which European integration could not proceed.

THE SYSTEM

The common price for wheat was called the target price (see Table 1). This price was not the target for every place in the Community, but only for the largest consumption area in the EEC, that is the city of Duisburg in West Germany. The target price for other areas being derived from this by deducting the transport costs involved in getting the wheat from that place to Duisburg. The derived target price in Rotterdam, largest grainport and gateway to Europe, is called the threshold price. This price is frequently much higher than the world market price (c.i.f. price)

Table 1. The EEC market regulation scheme, 1970.

Arrangements → Commodities ↓	Target price	Threshold price	Sluice gate price	Free at frontier price	Import levy	Supplementary levy	Import duty	Provision for market intervention	Provision for export refunds	Quota	Quality standards	Producers Organisation	Initial date	Date for unification[10]
Grain and grainproducts	□	□		□	□			□	□				1- 8-'62	1- 7-'67
Rice and riceproducts	□[1]	□		□	□			□[1]	□				1- 9-'64	1- 9-'67
Pigs and pigmeat			□		□	□			□				1- 8-'62	1- 7-'67
Poultry and eggs			□		□	□			□				1- 8-'62	1- 7-'67
Milk and dairyproducts	□[2]	□	□[3]	□	□			□[9]	□					29- 7-'68
Beef and veal				□	□		□	□	□	□[4]				29- 7-'68
Sugar and sugerbeets	□			□	□			□	□	□[5]			1- 7-'67	1- 7-'68
Oilseeds	□	□		□	□			□	□				1- 7-'67	1- 7-'67
Olive oil	□	□	□[6]	□	□		□	□	□				1-11-'66	1-11-'66
Fruit and vegetables								□	□	□[7]	□		1- 8-'62	1- 7-'68
Wine							□	□	□	□[8]	□	□	1- 8-'62	1-11-'69

1. In France and Italy; 2. Only in case of milk; 3. Guide price; 4. Levy free import quotum for frozen beef; 5. Production quotum; 6. Reference price; 7. Import quotum applicable only through a safe-guard clause procedure; 8. Import quotum; 9. Applicable for butter and skimmed milk powder; 10. Since the dates mentioned the EEC is unified. This means that for the inner EEC-trade there are no import-levies any longer and furthermore that for the trade with third countries there are uniform import-levies and export-refunds.

Rotterdam. It has been decided that this difference will be abridged by a levy on imported grain. If the world market price in Rotterdam (or any other place of entrance) would change the levy should be changed too, so we speak therefore about variable levies. In order to keep grain merchants and users of grain competitive this levy is refunded if the grain as such or in a processed form is exported again. The grain component of products like eggs, poultry, bacon etc. is charged with a levy too, so that these products can only enter the EEC at minimum or sluicegate prices, based on production costs which are related to the prices of domestically produced feed and feed/product conversion rates. There are periods of the year where there is not much international trade in (or import of) grain. Then the levies will not work, we cannot reach the target price then. To prevent this situation from happening an additional policy was implemented in the form of compulsory intervention by the central authorities. The farmers could sell any quantity of grain to these authorities for a guaranteed price, which was originally about seven per cent below the target price. This guaranteed price is called the intervention price. Intervention of course leads to storage of grain in the Community. In the beginning the necessary payments where made with the national treasuries. But France thought it to be safer for the realisation of the grain deal that the payments of levies or restitutions and for intervention were made on an European level. So we got a common fund called the European Agricultural Guarantee Fund.

The receipts of this fund in the form of levies were originally high enough to guarantee the payments for refunds or intervention, but in the course of years this has changed completely so that there came shortages in this fund, which were supplemented by payments out of the EEC budget. Each Member State had to contribute to this budget with a certain percentage of the value added tax. This percentage, increased in almost every year, is now

1.6 per cent. It is also an issue to change the basis of the contribution: instead of the value added tax some prefer the national incomes.

For milk and sugar the EEC developed a similar system. The sugar arrangement however was the first to be modified in the sense that there was no longer an unlimited guarantee, only for a limited amount of sugar ("A" quota) the full intervention price was payed, there was also "B" quota which got a lower guaranteed price. Together these quota were called "maximum" quota. Any sugar produced above the maximum was refered to as "C" sugar and did not get any price protection at all.

For beef and veal there is also a price protection, which in principle operates on the same basis only the terminology is different. We do not speak of the target price but of guide price. A complication is also that the intervention price is not the price at which the intervention buying takes place; this takes place at a buying in price. There are more complications but on the whole we have the same fundamental ideas. Only for oil seeds and olives we have a different system, because of GATT regulations. This means that imports can take place at world market levels. Protection takes place in a different form. Exporters of European oil seeds receive a supplement or restitution equal to the size of the desired price support. This supplement is also paid to manufactures of processed oil seeds grown in Europe. Which means that they are in a position to pay farmers the required price.

Even this rough sketch of the system sounds impressive and complicated. To be honest it is difficult and complicated and it became even more complicated because of additional rules for the solution of monetary problems and the problems that arose in relation to the so called substitutes and not to forget the surpluses.

The first complication to this already extended system arose as a result of the devaluation of the French franc in 1969 and the revaluation of the German mark which followed shortly after. The devaluation should have meant a change in the exchange rate against the Unit of Account, and this should have meant an increase in the price of agricultural products for the French consumer and higher incomes for French farmers. The French government did not think this advisable. The maintenance of the old rate of exchange against the European Unit of Account was however not possible just like that. The intervention price in EUA and in francs remained the same, but on exporting to Germany the picture was different. By offering the French wheat to the Intervention Boards in Germany the old price in EUA and in DM could be obtained, these marks could then be changed at any bank into more francs than before. Exports would thus be worthwhile. Supplies could become dangerously low in France and the German Intervention Boards would be flooded with French produce. Order in the market would be upset. To prevent this, a border levy equal to the size of gains from the exchange rate change was instituted between France and the other member states. Member states exporting to France were given a subsidy equal to that border levy. These payments at the border are called Monetary Compensatory Amounts. It was intended that these MCAs should only be temporary.

The revaluation of the DM caused similar problems. Adjusting the rates of exchange against the EUA implied less marks per EUA; meaning that German farmers would receive lower incomes. Such a reduction was not seen as desirable by the German government. The same price as before in EUA was paid on goods exported to Germany, and the same number of marks, but this could easily be exchanged for other currencies and exchange rate variation gains be made. In order to prevent difficulties arising in the market, imports were slowed down by introducing a border levy again equal to the exchange rate gains. Exports from Germany received a subsidy of the same magnitude.

Thus, both positive and negative MCAs were introduced. Since exchange rate variations continued and became in fact more frequent these MCAs remained in force, and were readjusted every week in periods of high currency unrest (floating). On the formation of the EMS the EUA was replaced by the ECU, which is a weighted average of the exchange rates or all the currencies of the member states. Every exchange rate change works through to the ECU and this affects the prices of agricultural products.

The level of the MCAs must be continually readjusted. The prices in national currency had a different trend in each of the member states. Uniformity of market prices has thus been lost.

The overall result of the agricultural policies and development in European farming was an increase in production at rather high and guaranteed price levels. This resulted in surpluses which created all kinds of problems: high budgetary expenses but not the desired level of incomes for farmers. In order to fulfill the clause calling for "reasonable incomes, reasonable prices and increases in productivity", an attempt was made to bring about a complete modernisation and restructuralisation of agriculture (Mansholt Plan, 1970). To achieve this, agricultural employment had to be reduced by about 50%, farm-area by about 7% and some capital be transferred to other production areas. The remaining agricultural resources should be organized into large modern units. On such farms farmers would obtain reasonable incomes at the existing price levels, without having undesirable effects on total supply or the consumer be forced to pay too high prices. International trade would also not be negatively affected. With this in mind, the Mansholt plan was born; however, because of enormous political opposition, no effective large scale structural measures were actually undertaken.

Guidelines on measures for pensioning off and re-educating farmers, and for interest subsidies on some forms of modernisation investment (all to be conducted on a national level) was all that emerged. To finance these measures a 'Guidance Section' of the European Fund was set up.

It became clear that the hill-farmers could never receive reasonable incomes via the guaranteed price system without over-riding the stated aim regarding prices to consumers and meaning unnecessarily high farm incomes in other areas. But it was not always socially desirable to leave these people without additional governmental support. It was felt that neither the social environment nor the rural beauty (through erosion) of the hilly areas should be allowed to be destroyed. Thus, the so called hill and mountain farm regulation came into being.

Clearly the community responsibility for the financing of the policy has become an increasingly important element in the discussion regarding market regulation. The need emerged to limit the applicability of price guarantees somewhat, by such diverse measures as premiums on non-delivery of milk, premiums on cattle slaughter, consumer subsidies for butter, milk powder and school milk. Additionally, in the case of milk and grain, lower intervention prices apply for quantities, over and above a certain production ceiling. This reduction of the marginal price is called the 'Coresponsibility levy'.[8]

When this proved to be insufficient, a stop on production was invented. It said that the intervention price would only be paid for a certain quotum (about the 1983-production level), any farmer producing more than this amount will be penalized with a super levy of about 75 per cent of the intervention price. The rules for this quotum system are in themselves too complicated to deal with in these few pages.

We have also problems concerning the so called substitutes. The grain substitutes are best known although there are now also substitutes for sugar, milk, beef etc. A well-known grain substitute was tapioca. At the time this was an insignificant product on world markets; it was more expensive than grains, but as a result of the levies imported grains became dearer than tapioca. It was therefore an attractive proposition to feed processors to use tapioca rather than grains. Pig production became cheaper this way and an expansion of this production was the result. This reduced the use of grains of course, for which there was a large intervention storage or even a surplus. So it was decided to restrict the use and import of tapioca. This was rather embarrassing because the exporters are developing countries e.g. Thailand. It was decided that this country should not export more than a certain quantity, to prohibit the export completely was impossible for obvious political reasons.

Since article 39 of the Treaty of Rome seems to place so much importance on the improvement of agricultural productivity one should perhaps expect a policy to promote agricultural technology or to improve the structure of agriculture.

There have been some measures for the improvement of land allocation and of markets and marketing channels. But these guidance measures are of limiting importance both technically and financially. In 1984 for example whilst 27 249 million ECU were allocated from the European Fund only 675 million ECU were in the Guidance Section whereas the Guarantee Section got 18333 million ECU. The policies regarding the technical development of agriculture are left to the national authorities. The system was therefore fundamentally a market and price policy with an unlimited guarantee. This has been changed first with sugar and later on with milk whereas there are proposals to limit the intervention and/or production for grains too. The main issue of the Common Agricultural Policy in the last part of the 1980s is therefore the limiting of the guarantee for agricultural prices in one way or another. The unification in 1992 will need some further adaptations. It is questionable for example whether the MCAs can be maintained. The global policies (vis-à-vis the U.S. and the developing countries, the UNCTAD and GATT) for grains, beef, sugar, etc. will require also some changes in the Common Agricultural Policy. So the system will be in a state of constant repair and change.

The main aspects of the CAP are therefore the changes in the price level decided upon by the Council of Ministers, see Table 2.

RESULTS AND PROBLEMS

The EEC has a common market policy and a common price level for many agricultural products, but if we look at the price level in national prices (applying exchange rates) we will see that the price levels and their trends differ greatly between member countries. The differences are as great as before the Treaty of Rome. These differences can exist because of that system of special levies and subsidies between the Member States called Monetary Compensatory Amounts. The various price levels, however, have always been above world market price levels and were attractive for France. France could, therefore, profit from the grain deal: it could increase its share of the European market (see Table 3) in exchange for a German industrial expansion. The French did

Table 2. Average change in agricultural prices (in per cent), decided upon by the Council of Ministers in various years.

EC—6	%	EC—9	%	EC—10	%
1968—69	−1.3	1973—74	6.1	1982—83	10.3
1969—70	0	1974—75	15.5	1983—84	4.3
1970—71	0.5	1975—76	8.6	1984—85	−0.4
1971—72	4	1976—77	9.1	1985—86	0.1
1972—73	4.7	1977—78	4.9	1986—87	−0.3
		1978—79	2.4	1987—88	−0.2
		1979—80	1.2	1988—89	−0.1
		1980—81	4.9		
		1981—82	9.3		

Source: (11).

Table 3. The expansion of the French agricultural market share.

	1960	1967	1980	
Grains	23	32	48	mln tons
	(33)	(36)	(40)	%
Sugar	19	12	26	mln tons
	(33)	(20)	(32)	%
Milk	23	27	32	mln tons
	(26)	(28)	(28)	%

indeed obtain a larger agricultural market, although they were faced with some competition from the Dutch who had a high agricultural productivity and an excellent geographical position. Because of the German political pressure the price level was high, which prevented the French also from having an even larger market share. The high prices lead to a high effective rate of protection for the main agricultural products like wheat, meat, cheese or butter.

It is said that the CAP has only one instrument — the common price level — whereas the Treaty of Rome lays down many targets. Formally, the CAP would therefore be an illogical construction; it would only be logical to have a separate instrument for each target or political end. But should we look at the CAP in this way? The real and main target of the CAP was to obtain French co-operation in European policy. Market and price policies have realized this goal, though with some clashes of interest. The so-called goals of the CAP, for example as formulated in article 39 of the Treaty, can better be seen as limiting conditions (or restrictions), indicating other interests to be considered in realizing the agricultural policy.

Consumers, for example, were apprehensive of too high price levels for agricultural products. Is it true that the CAP has consumer's interests at heart and that prices are not too high? The facts are that prices at farm gate have risen less than retail prices. Without the CAP the purchasing power of the consumers would have been higher. They have been paying about 2.3 percent of national income as income transfer to farmers (see Table 4), but without CAP there would have been a similar (national) transfer to income, so we should only look at the additional aspects which are difficult to estimate. The consumers also had some interest in supply and in self-sufficiency. The achievement of self-sufficiency is remarkable. For almost all products the degree of self-sufficiency has increased considerably since the inception of the EEC, often to figures exceeding 100 percent! As a consequence, ample supplies have been available for consumers, but at a cost, for in their role as taxpayers, consumers have also paid out large sums. This has taken place in a period in which all countries have been experiencing serious problems with government finances. So when expenditures of the EC reached the limits of the "own resources" (in 1982/83) we had a problem but also a political possibility to change the CAP.

Foreign consumers have benefited from the CAP because food has become cheap and this may have improved welfare in some countries although foreign exporters have suffered: they complain of dumping. For developing countries the repercussions are mixed: industrialization policies benefit, but those countries that give priority to agricultural development have suffered. The external (net) welfare effect of the EC agricultural price policy is difficult to assess and is still a much debated issue.[12]

Some politicians and economists were afraid of the high real costs of protection: too many resources in agriculture, a bad structure and low productivity. According to article 39, this should be prevented and in this the agricultural policies have been successful. Since the Treaty of Rome was signed, there has been an enormous outflow of agricultural labour (about 4% per year), an increase in farm size and a rise in technical productivity (by between 3 to 5% per year: this rate is as good as can be found in industry).

It is true, however, that as a consequence of price protection, labour (that could better have been employed in other parts of the economy) was retained in agriculture — at the expense of the domestic product of the EC. So there are real costs involved with the CAP. These are not more than 0.5 percent of domestic product, set Table 4. In the period of growth 1965—1975 this was not a large burden, particularly when it is remembered that without the CAP we would have had national price policies that would also have had their real costs. The additional real costs of the CAP are therefore around 0.2 percent of domestic product.

The real benefits of free trade between Member States was according to Scitovsky[7] perhaps 0.1 to 0.5 percent of domestic product. In comparison with these benefits the costs of agricultural protection were high. This could only be accepted as the

Table 4. Recent estimates of EC transfers and costs as a result of agricultural to gross domestic product and on a per person basis.[1]

Period	Cost to consumers	Cost to taxpayers	Total cost to consumers and taxpayers	Cost to the economy weight
	As a percentage of gross domestic product			
Average 1973—83	1.3	1.0	2.3	0.30
	Per person, in 1982 values (ECU)			
Average 1973—83	112	86	198	27

[1] After allowance for the estimated effect of EC support policies on world market prices for major agricultural products.
Source: (8).

political and "dynamic" benefits were considerable. It is not surprising that protests against the CAP became serious again in the
1980s when the economic growth, the dynamic benefits of integration and even the political benefits seemed too small, whereas
the trade problems were mounting e.g. by not following the price-
lead of the U.S. in the international grainmarkets.

The real cost of the CAP should not be confused with the
budget costs which are impressive indeed in absolute terms (see
Table 5 and 6), but in relative terms it increased from 0.50
percent in 1973 to about 0.95 percent of national product[9] in
1985, which can be not such a burden as sometimes is suggested,
but the increases are perhaps disturbing.

Farmers were afraid of a loss in their position. In general the
relative position of farmers increased. Farmer's income grew
considerably in the 1960s and 1970s but there still is a disparity
of incomes.[1] It is remarkable that this income depends heavily
(for about 50 percent) on a transfer of income, indicating the
importance of the protection element of the CAP.

So there really have been problems: real costs, income transfers,

Table 5. Guarantee expenditure by economy category (x million ECU).

Year	Storage	Aids	Other	Co-respon-sibility receipts from milk	Export refunds	Total guarantee expendi-ture
1979	1658	3779	116	− 94	4982	10441
1980	1617	3928	298	−223	5695	11315
1981	1631	4343	436	−178	5209	11141
1982	1818	5468	603	−537	5054	12406
1983	2893	7281	712	−527	5560	15920
1984	3583	7942	1130	−972	6718	18401

Source: (8).

Table 6. Community revenue and expenditure (x million ECU).

Item	1974	1976	1978	1980	1982	1984
Revenue						
Customs duties	2737	4064	4391	5906	6815	7884
Agricultural levies	330	1164	2279	2002	2228	3172
Value-added tax				7259	12000	14377
Other	1669	2765	5507	899	197	1816
Total	5036	7993	12177	16066	21241	27249
Expenditure						
Agriculture:						
— Guarantee Section	3278	5365	9279	11306	12406	18333
— Guidance Section	128	218	324	601	548	675
Total	4516	7238	11973	16290	20012	27249
Agriculture's share	75	77	80	73	65	70

Source: (8).

budgetary costs, income disparity, disturbance of international trade or development policies. Nevertheless, the EC has obtained six new members: Greece, U.K., Eire, Denmark, Spain and Portugal. The recent entrance of two new members (Spain and Portugal) will lead to additional problems in all these areas.

SOLUTIONS AND PROSPECTS

Looking back, we can say that the European policy to arrive at peace, stability and democracy in Europe has been a priority. The policies of economic integration can be seen as a means of achieving this goal. The agricultural policy is part of this policy and is also a concrete example of the complicated and costly means of achieving that goal. The main element is protection of farm income.

The situation is now very different from that in the 1950s. We are no longer concerned with reconstruction and reconciliation; East-West relations are also different.

There is no fear of food shortages anymore. We are concentrating more on daily, technical problems than on dealing with high ideals. Nevertheless, we have grave social and economic problems and it is surprising that there are not more common actions against unemployment, environmental destruction, energy problems, or for scientific research and for strategies of development. The entry into the EEC of Spain and Portugal reminded us to the idealistic desire to strengthen democracy in Europe. But again, even these important policies are overshadowed by a large number of more or less technical problems concerning vegetables, grain, wine, money and all kinds of foreign relations in the Mediterranean.

I believe that France and the northern areas of the EEC are now in a similar position as Germany was in 1957. Spain and Portugal have special agricultural interests, just as the founder EEC members now have industrial interests. It is interesting indeed to "swap markets". It is even questionable whether France did in fact have such a large economic interest in grain exports as was said at the time;[2] but nowadays even France is an industrial nation and should give Spain a chance, in exchange for participation in large industrial market. The CAP has the historical rôle of improving and accelerating economic and political integration and should not become a brake on these policies.

Many proposals for new policies have been put forward and some have indeed been incorporated in the CAP. I believe it is unwise to continue changing policies each season. There are still many alternatives open to the CAP. Let us consider some major examples.

One of the oldest alternatives is a structural policy. Price levels could be lower if we had a modern well-structured agriculture. Thus in the late 1960s Commissioner Mansholt proposed a plan to achieve this in agriculture. The idea was to accelerate the outmigration of rural labour and the modernization of agriculture. This plan ran into much opposition because of its flaws. For example, it had a low rate of return, needed a large budget, did not consider the unfavourable social consequences of migration and it disregarded the vested interests of the agricultural lobby. Today we could also use a better organized agriculture, but a new Mansholt Plan would be no wise policy because an additional outflow of labour from agriculture would be unprofitable because of unemployment and the modernisation of agriculture would also lead to more production and more surpluses, which is also unprofitable. Additional structural measures are therefore not the solution.

An effective measure is to decrease price levels or levels of protection. The high price levels are the real cause of surpluses. Many would gain from lower price, but farming and some agribusiness would not. The income position of farmers is an important aspect of agricultural policies in Europe and this policy line is therefore not generally acceptable in real politics e.g. when applied to cereals in 1985 it created much political tension in the Community. Comparable proposals that have been considered have involved increases in import prices, especially of feed foodstuffs, which have always led to an intensive political debate with no results.

To have the advantages of low prices but also to maintain income protection and the social position of farmers, Professor van Riemsdijk proposed a direct income payment system in which the loss of income resulting from the lower prices would be compensated for by direct income payments to farmers. These payments would only be made for a limited period of time, at most twenty years, and only to farmers up to 65 years of age. This would give a stimulus to improve farming, because after that transitional period low prices would rule the agricultural economy and to survive, farmers would need larger and modern farms. This plan was also debated but rejected, because it also had a low rate of return, needed a large budget and would have led to large-scale migration, with all its social and political repercussions. Today, all these problems would still follow such a policy to an even greater degree, because an additional outmigration is not at all profitable and any increase in the budget for agriculture would meet great political opposition.

Another method is to restrict production by imposing production quotas per country and per farmer. There is a large range of possibilities in this field. The super levy system now in use in the dairy sector is perhaps the best known example. It is a purely technical measure.

It restricts production and therefore decreases the budget costs of the CAP but without the basic systematic improvements that the above mentioned alternative policies promised to give. The restrictive measures that in fact have been taken for sugar and milk and to a lesser degree also the production ceiling for grains have changed the CAP system from an unlimited guarantee to a limited one. This is already a considerable change when we realize how strongly the farmers are organized compared with all other interest groups involved.

Interesting proposals are also to take marginal land out of agricultural production and use it for timber production or for recreation. The difficulty with this policy idea is to find in fact this marginal land. In the Netherlands e.g. you cannot find any considerable area of this type of land and it is said that timber production is not profitable and therefore not an attractive alternative to milk production. But in several other regions it could indeed be a splendid idea, to increase alternative production. The problem with labour extensive products like timber is that you have to find new means to protect employment now found in the CAP.

This would require an additional social policy. It is interesting to note that such policies of new uses of agricultural land have a positive effect on the environment.

Each of these measures has its variations. So in theory, there are many alternative proposals for solving the CAP problems. Among economists there is a strong tendency to try to find the optimal instrument in that series of solutions by estimating the total net effect on welfare of the Community each instrument has, and selecting the highest-scoring measure. The difficulty with this procedure, based on Professor Tinbergen's theory of economic policy,[5] is, that there is in fact no social welfare function or no such function can be specified and estimated. So it is no use looking for an instrument or measure that will lead to the maximum value of this function.[4] This method can only be applied to individual or partial preferences but will not indicate the *social* preferences of a nation or the Community as a whole. The real selection can therefore only be done by other, that is political means. This conclusion is too often overlooked by economists.

It is a pity that political science has no empirically tested theory on political decision-making on this level. So they too cannot explain why some policies are applied or rejected. What we can say is that the political selection process in Europe is dominated by the "unanimity rule" in the Council of Ministers (this is a result of President de Gaulle's policy towards the EEC in 1965). This Council is a kind of coalition government of the EEC: ministers one of each member state working towards common decisions. The bartering of votes between them is an obvious way of reaching agreements. To reach unanimity will require more strength and more exchange or trade-offs than simple majority rule would require. Because in practice this Council only deals with agricultural affairs and not all types of other affairs (as a national cabinet must do) the political bargaining will lead to ever more measures in the agricultural field, each time making agricultural policy more expensive not only in the seventies but even in recent years when the problems were well known to the public, see Table 7.

So if we could find more common policies (e.g. for energy, environment, unemployment, research) and if we could really apply majority rule we could get easier and cheaper political solutions for agriculture too.

The CAP has a very introvert character, because it is mainly the representatives of farmers and of the ministers of agriculture who are involved in the decision-making process in Brussels. The only opportunity for others to influence the process is in case the "own means" of the Community fall too short. We see then new proposals for financing the Community or to reform the CAP but they hardly succeed in really changing and improving the situation.[6] Consumers behave as if their interest in the CAP is not so

Table 7. EC budget and agricultural expenditure in recent years (x million ECU).

Year	Total EC budget	Total for agriculture	Guarantee	Structure
1982	20705	13055	12405	605
1983	24807	16539	15811	728
1984	27208	19022	18346	676
1985	28085	20463	19744	719
1986	35174	22910	22137	774
1987	35783	23876	22968	908
1988	43820	29998	28795	1203
1989	45030	29758	28323	1434

Source: EC Commission, Brussels.

high as for producers such as farmers and farmsuppliers. An enlarged EEC cannot continue with its agricultural policies in the same way as it did before the entry of Spain and Portugal. Continuing to increase price levels is leading us into grave problems internationally, because we invite trade difficulties with the USA and nationally because of budgetary problems (including fraud) and unequal treatment of farmers and other businessmen in distress. We must realize also that small farmers, with only small means of production (of which there are many especially in Southern Europe) can never be given a reasonable income by price policies only. High prices lead also to large income differences within agriculture and have a tendency to lead to high rents and land prices. We will need a freeze on prices and production for some time. To prevent social problems we could try to secure a reasonable income for farmers by introducing i.e. income deficiency payments. This would fit the new GATT proposals to liberalise world trade. Agricultural protection becomes then more and more a social measure for farmers.

These social measures could even be part of the national social policy and therefore be completely financed out of the national budget. If this is done we will have reached the watershed between the economic and the social aspects of agricultural policies. In future, the social aspect could better be dealt with separately. This idea has become part of the new proposals of Commissioner Andriessen to reform the Common Agricultural Policy as formulated in his Green-book. These proposals are now at the start of the political decision making process. Experience with former reform proposals show that it will be not simple and easy. (In fact the German government started such a policy to be effective in the second half of the year 1987). But this time it must have positive results, otherwise the Common Agricultural Policy will become a breaking point in European policies.

52

REFERENCES

1. Meester, G & D. Strijker, *Het Europese landbouwbeleid. Voorbij de scheidslijn van zelfvoorziening.* Wetenschappelijke Raad voor het Regeringsbeleid, Den Haag, 1985.
2. Harvey, D.R., "National Interests and the CAP", *Food Policy*, August 1982.
3. Tracy, M., "Agriculture in Western Europe", *Challenge and Response*, Granada, London, 1982.
4. Van den Noort, P.C., "The problem of optimum policy choice in European agriculture", *Neth. J. of Agr.Sci.* 31 (1983), pp. 93—97.
5. Tinbergen, J., *On the theory of economic policy*, North-Holland, Amsterdam, 1952.
6. Pelkmans, J. (ed), "Can the CAP be reformed?", *IEAP*, Maastricht, 1985.
7. Scitovsky, Tibor, *Economic Theory and Western European Integration*, Unwin. London, 1958, p. 67.
8. *Agricultural Policies in the European Community, Their Origins, Nature and Effects on Production and Trade.* Policy Monograph No. 2., Bureau of Agricultural Economics, Canberra, 1985.
9. Spaventa, L., L. Koopmans et. al., "The future of Community Finance", CEPS—Papers No. 30, Brussels 1986.
10. S. J. Wells, *International Economics* (Allen and Unwin), London 1973.
11. Gilbert, A., "Twintig jaar Europese landbouw, Groen Europa", *Landbouwbulletin* 217, Brussels 1987.
12. Hoogh, J. de, "Agricultural policies and the third world", *Tijdschr. v. Sociaal wetensch. onderz. v.d. Landb.* (2) 1987, pp. 68—81.

Fiscal policy in the EEC —
some recent developments

WALTER HAHN

Although some four years have passed since Professor Prest wrote his article "On fiscal policy in the EEC", the Community's critical situation in the area of fiscal affairs has remained the same: The EC is still living at the edge of bankruptcy.

Most people who follow current affairs will remember the years when Mrs. Thatcher constantly pressed for budgetary reforms in general and a British rebate from the common Budget in particular. During those years — 1979 to 1983 — the EC was in danger of running out of money from one day to the next. But it was not until June 1984 that the European Council agreed at its Fontainebleau Summit to increase the Community's won resources:
— The VAT ceiling was raised from 1% to 1.4%.
— Britain was promised a rebate from the Budget, set at 66% of the difference between Britain's VAT payments to the Community and its share of Community spending; in order to limit the financial burden on the Germans, it was also decided that West Germany should pay only half of its normal contribution towards this British rebate (*EC Bulletin* 6, 1984).
But, as insiders were aware from the start, the additional finances could not afford the EEC even temporary relief from budgetary pressures. The Community's spending on the Common Agricultural Policy continued to escalate, and the 1986 enlargement

53

P. Coffey (ed.), Main Economic Policy Areas of the EEC — Toward 1992. pp. 53—61.
© *1990 Kluwer Academic Publishers, Dordrecht — Printed in the Netherlands.*

placed a second burden on the Budget. Therefore it was not surprising that in 1986, the year the Fontainebleau Agreement went fully into force, the Community's expenditure already once more exceeded revenue by about 3.5 b ECU. Since the EEC is in general not allowed to borrow or to run deficits, the Commission could save the Community from bankruptcy only by dubious accounting tricks: deferring spending, not writing down the value of stocks, disguising deficits by putting them off to later years.

Such devices obviously cannot work forever. Moreover, the new common policies mentioned in the Single European Act, and particularly the EC's ambitious program on Completing the Internal Market by 1992, will require additional resources at the Community level in the coming years. Budgetary reform, therefore, is essential. The Commission has already put forward some proposals (*EC Bulletin*, Supplement 1, 1987). On the revenue side, the main features of the Commission's approach to budgetary reform are as follows:

— Customs duties and agricultural levies would remain a part of the EC's own resources. But since customs barriers are declining at a multinational level while, at the same time, Europe's self-sufficiency in agricultural products is increasing, their relative importance (today they account for about one third of the EC's revenue) will continue to fall in future.

— The member states would pay to the Budget a jointly fixed percentage of the difference between the national GDP and the VAT base (this includes particularly public expenditure, investment and the surplus of exports over imports). Simultaneously, the Commission would accept a reduction in the VAT contributions from 1.4% today to 1%.

— In addition to the levies mentioned above, the EC should be free to introduce a fifth one (which has not yet been defined) before 1992.

— All levies together should not exceed 1.4% of the Community's GDP.

Since the EC's own resources (1.4% of VAT plus customs duties and agricultural levies) currently account for only about 1% of GDP, the Commission's program means a quite remarkable increase in contributions to the Budget. But this increased financing alone would not be sufficient to finance the policies of tomorrow. Therefore, a restructuring of the expenditure side of the Budget is also badly needed:

— By means of greater "budgetary discipline", the Commission aims to reduce spending on CAP from over 60% of the total Budget today to about 50% in 1992. "Discipline" the member states already pledged to in 1984. At that time, however, it had little effect because the Finance Council was not able to get the Ministers of Agriculture under its control. This time, therefore, the Commission would like to be armed with so-called "automatic stabilizers", that would empower it to impose price cuts, production thresholds or extra levies on production whenever spending looks like going over the limit.

— Parallel to cutting back expenditure on CAP, the Commission sees a need to increase the Regional, Social and Agricultural Structural Fund from today's 16% of the total budget to about 3% in 1992, to spend more on research (about 3% in 1992) and, last but not least, to leave some room for new policies to be defined in the coming years (around 5% of the 1992 Budget).

Setting aside details and taking the concept as a whole, the Commission's approach to budgetary reform points in the right direction. Whenever the responsibility for a certain policy (e.g., research, environmental protection or transport) is shifted upward from the national level to the Community, it seems fairly reasonable also to shift the corresponding fund (i.e., the research fund, etc.) from the national to the EC budget. But while the member states appreciate the need for the first step, they are not yet prepared to take the second.

Nevertheless, reluctance on the part of national governments and parliaments to give additional finances to Brussels should not be able to stop the further development of the Community. Even the EC of 1992 can survive with a Budget of, say, 1% or 1.2% of GDP. In order to do so, the Community will have to restrict itself, wherever possible, to controlling (or, more diplomatically: "coordinating") the spending of national funds rather than to spending its own resources.

Fiscal policy in the EC does not only deal with the Community's common budget, it is also concerned with harmonizing the fiscal systems of the member states. Fiscal harmonization is not an end in itself; it is rather a means of achieving certain common goals of the Community's Neutrality in competition or the abolition of the EC's internal border controls — both objectives being essential elements of the Community's internal market program — require, for instance, that the indirect taxes of the EC's member states are harmonized to some extent (see Prest).

As far as neutrality in competition is concerned, most of the major problems have already been resolved. The Council's decision of 1967 to introduce a VAT in all the member states and that of 1977 to harmonize the VAT's basis of assessment have ensured (apart from some minor distortions which still exist) the neutrality of general sales taxes. In the area of excise duties (except those on cigarettes) the Council did not take any action at all. But since the late 1970s, the Commission has taken an increasing number of cases to the European Court of Justice, alleging that certain member states have not yet fulfilled their obligations under Article 95 of the Treaty of Rome. As a result of these initiatives, the Luxembourg judges ruled that France had to equalize the tax rates levied on cognac and whisky (1980), that Britain had to reduce her duty on wine relative to the duty on beer (1983), etc. (Easson 1981 and Easson 1984).

So far, practically nothing has been achieved with regard to the abolition of the so-called fiscal frontiers within the EC. Only very recently have things slowly started to move. In particular, the Commission's White Paper of June 1985 and Completing the Internal market (Commission 1985) and the Single European Act recalled the continuing existence of border checks, neglected since the early 1970s, to the minds of European ministers and bureaucrats. The far-reaching program originally presented by the Brussels authorities and now embodied in the Single European Act calls for the abolition of all fiscal and non-fiscal controls at the EC's internal borders by 1992. Since the abolition of border checks requires alignment of the indirect tax rates levied in the member states, the Commission put forward the following proposals in August 1987 (COM (87) 320—328):

— All member states should levy two VAT rates; the Commission suggests that the standard rate should lie within the range of 14% to 20% and the reduced rate between 4% and 9%, arguing that tax differentials of up to 6% between neighbouring countries would not significantly distort trade.

— After the abolition of tax rebates for exports/taxes levied on imports in intra-Community trade, a central clearing-house should redistribute VAT revenue between the member states according to the destination principle.

— The excise duties' basis of assessment must be standardized throughout the Community; the tax rates levied on alcoholic beverages (excluding VAT) should be the same in all states, while those levied on tobacco (including VAT) should lie within a range of 2% of each other (Table 1, 2).

There are three major problems which make it unlikely that the Draft Directions put forward by the Commission will be adopted before 1992:

— The Commission's proposals have considerable budgetary implications for most of the member states. Problems will arise particularly in Denmark and Ireland, two countries which would suffer a heavy loss in tax revenue (Table 3).

Table 1. VAT Rates (%) April 1987.

Country	Standard	Reduced	Increased
Belgium	19	1/6	25/33
Denmark	22	—	—
France	18.6	2.1/4/5.5/7	33.3
Greece	18	6	36
Ireland	25	0/2.4/10	—
Italy	18	2/9	38
Luxembourg	12	3/6	—
Netherlands	20	6	—
Portugal	16	8	30
Spain	12	6	33
U.K.	15	0	—
W. Germany	14	7	—

Source: COM (87) 320, 4 August 1987.
Note: Several member states (e.g., Denmark and the U.K.) levy, usually at the wholesale stage, supplementary taxes on certain items like cars, TVs etc. Those levies have the same effect as an increased VAT rate.

Table 2. Examples of excise duties (ECU) March 1985.

Country	20 cigarettes	1 litre of beer	1 litre of wine	0.75 litre of 40% spirits	1 litre of prem. petrol
Belgium	0.83	0.13	0.33	3.78	0.25
Denmark	1.96	0.65	1.35	9.58[1]	0.28
France	0.31	0.03	0.03	3.37	0.36
Greece	0.28	0.22	0.00	0.16	0.29
Ireland	1.14	1.14	2.74	7.84	0.36
Italy	0.57	0.18	0.00	0.75	0.49
Luxembourg	0.54	0.06	0.13	2.54	0.20
Netherlands	0.74	0.23	0.33	3.79	0.28
U.K.	1.25	0.70	1.60	7.70	0.29
W. Germany	1.02	0.07	0.00	3.43	0.23

Source: Commission's White Paper on Completing the Internal Market, June 1985.
Note: 1. Estimated average.

Table 3. Gain/Loss in Tax Revenue Implied by the Commission's 1987 Proposals Estimate in % GDP.

Luxembourg	+7.6	Italy	± 0
Portugal	+3.0	Belgium	± 0
Spain	+2.8	Netherlands	± 0
Greece	+1.1	France	−0.2
United Kingdom	+0.7	Ireland	−1.6
W. Germany	+0.3	Denmark	−4.8

Source: Neue Züricher Zeitung, September 7, 1987.

— The structure and rates of excise duties vary widely from one country to another. Any attempt to harmonize them will not only affect the general public but also homogeneous and well organized groups of producers with a strong interest in preserving the status quo (e.g., wine growers in the southern part of Europe and brewers in the North).

— A great many technical problems have to be resolved, the clearing-house being only one of them. The cooperation between the national tax authorities urgently required to prevent tax fraud after fiscal frontiers have been abolished is a second major issue.

Although there are no grounds for being overly optimistic about the near future, there is a way to achieve some progress nevertheless. From today's perspective only a step-by-step approach appears to be feasible: step-by-step in the sense that the EC will first try to simplify border controls (along the lines demonstrated by the Benelux countries) with the aim of abolishing them altogether once tax rates are sufficiently aligned; and step-by-step in the sense that some countries will go ahead with abolishing fiscal frontiers while others, e.g., Denmark, Ireland and the United Kingdom, follow later (a Europe of two or three speeds).

Completing the Internal Market is often misunderstood as simply eliminating all restrictions on the free movement of goods across borders. But the Internal Market means much more. It also implies liberalizing the exchange of services (e.g., transport, banking and insurance) and the exchange of capital. In most countries, services are subject to particular taxes which will also have to be harmonized eventually. Since the Court of Justice has ruled that transport within the EC must be liberalized by 1992, the carriers' interest groups, for instance, have started pressing their national governments to go ahead with the harmonization of taxes levied on vehicles. The free flow of capital, on the other hand, is heavily affected by the national systems of corporation income tax. Here we find no pressure similar to that exerted by the carriers. This might explain why the systems as well as the rates of corporation tax still vary widely within the Community (Table 4) and why

Table 4. Corporation Tax System, Rates etc. 1986.

Country	System	Corporation Tax Rate %	Imputation Credit (if relevant) %
Netherlands	Separate	42	0
Luxembourg	Separate	40[1]	0
Spain	Imputation	35	18.57
Denmark	Imputation	50	25
Belgium	Imputation	45[1]	40.87
Ireland	Imputation	50[1]	53.85
France	Imputation	45	61.11
U.K.	Imputation	35[1]	75.81
Greece	(Imputation)[2]	49	100
Portugal	(Imputation)[2]	34.2 to 47.2	100
W. Germany	Imputation	56/36[3]	100
Italy	Imputation	46.368[4]	100

Source: Information from the German Ministry of Finance and own calculations.

Notes: 1. Reduced Rates are applied to low income.
2. In Greece and Portugal distributed profits are not subject to corporation tax what in fact is equivalent to a 100% imputation credit.
3. The 36% rate is levied on distributed profits.
4. Sum of central and local taxes.

discussion on harmonization has practically come to a standstill since the early 1980s.

BIBLIOGRAPHY

Andel, N. (1983), Direction of Tax Harmonization in the EEC, in: Cnossen, S. (ed.), *Comparative Tax Studies*, Amsterdam: North-Holland 1983, p. 295.
Commission (1985), *White Paper on Completing the Internal Market*, June 1985.
Easson, A. J. (1981), "Fiscal Discrimination: New Perspectives on Article 95 of the EEC Treaty;", in: *Common Market Law Review*, 18 (1981) p. 521.
Easson, A. J. (1984), "Cheaper Wine or Dearer Beer?", Article 95 again, in: *European Law Review*, 9 (1984) p. 57.
Hahn, W. (1987), "Steuerpolitische Willensbildungs-prozesse in der EG — Das Beispiel der Umsatzsteuer-harmonisierung", Saarbrücken: Dissertation Universität des Saarlandes 1987.
Simons, A. L. C. (1981), "Simplification of VAT Procedures in Intra-Community Trade", in: *Intertax*, 1981, p. 375.

Regional policy

WILHELM MOLLE

Introduction

European regional policy has developed in a specific *context*. The EC was created with the objective to step up efficiency and stimulate economic growth by integrating the national markets of goods and production factors. That the ensuing structural changes (relocation of economic activities, changing composition of sectoral activity) could have consequences for certain sectors of society, was expected. The most vulnerable groups were concentrated, on the one hand, in particular regions or even countries (geographical dimension) and on the other in particular sectors of the labour force (social dimension). To gather the benefits of integration, the EC has taken upon itself to compensate these groups for their losses and help them adapt to the new situation. In that spirit, redistribution policies, in practice the social and regional policies of the EC, were developed. While the EC has been pledged to social policy ever since its creation, its regional policy did not really take off until after the first enlargement of the EC. Real political commitment to regional policy was not achieved until the 1972 Conference of the European Council. That Paris Conference called for vigorous Community action to diminish regional imbalances, and recognised the need to create a Regional Fund.

63

P. Coffey (ed.), Main Economic Policy Areas of the EEC — Toward 1992. pp. 63—99.
© *1990 Kluwer Academic Publishers, Dordrecht — Printed in the Netherlands.*

With the enlargement to the EC12, regional disparities have increased and so has policy attention.

The present chapter deals in some detail with European (EC12) Regional Policy. Its *structure* will be as follows.

First we will discuss why a regional policy is pursued, explaining how regional disequilibria occur, and giving the economic and social justification of doing something about them. The next section describes the regional policy actually pursued by the EC, proper attention being given to each of its four dimensions.

The highly important question analysed next is what the effects of the policy are. We will treat its economic effectiveness as well as the more psychological aspects of its contribution to welfare. Finally, we will draw some conclusions and try to envisage how regional policy may evolve in the near future, under the influence of such new developments as the completion of the internal market.

FOUNDATIONS OF REGIONAL POLICY

Theoretical foundations

Within every country there are differences in economic development among regions. These differences are more pronounced in some countries than in others. They are mostly measured by such indicators as the concentration of people and economic activities, the level of income per capita, the productivity by working person, and the availability and accessibility of environmental goods, cultural infrastructure, leisure activities, etc.

The theory of regional development and historical analysis (e.g. Pollard 1981) indicate that these differences are the result not of incidental factors, but of a complex interplay of mutually dependent factors which in the past have always collectively determined the location of economic activities and people. Geographical facts can be thought of, for instance the situation at the mouth of a river, or economic-technological factors that may have governed the cost relations of the production at various places, demographic factors that have influenced the volume and total growth of the population, etc. Such factors change constantly, but not necessarily towards a better equilibrium.

Regional equilibrium is a central element in literature, which of course mentions other elements besides (Richardson, 1973, Paelinck and Nijkamp, 1976). *Most theories of regional development start from regions in a national setting.*

Theories of regional development start with the classical school.

The basic assumptions of *(neo)classical* theory of regional development were: (a) free competition and entry, (b) full employment of factors of production, (c) full mobility of labour and capital, (d) equal technology (Paelinck and Nijkamp, 1976). Classical theory states that under such conditions the system tends to equalise wages and rents across space, and to a state of equilibrium. However, in practice the conditions of neoclassical theory are never fulfilled and consequently the equalitarian end effect is not assured either. For one thing, labour and capital are not in practice completely mobile, so that factor incomes can become higher in one region than in another. Moreover, regions do not all start from an equilibrium position; historical and geographical factors have produced uneven situations, which in themselves put regions in different starting positions for future developments.

International trade theory, based on the Heckscher-Ohlin theorem, can be transposed to regions; it then states that a region tends to specialise in the production and exportation of commodities whose production requires large amounts of factors in relatively abundant supply there, while importing commodities which the production of which it is at a comparative disadvantage. However, once more theory is at odds with reality; the basic assumptions are not fulfilled in practice: transportation costs are not zero, production functions are not identical in different regions, there are economies and diseconomies of scale, and competition is not perfect (Vanhove and Klaassen, 1987).

Another theory is that of the *export base*, by which regional growth depends on the region's capacity to export products to other regions. The more a region is specialised in products that are much in demands, the faster it grows. The lower the income elasticity for its products, the slower its growth. Differences in regional growth would thus spring from initial economic structures, which in turn can be attributed to historical and present comparative advantages (for instance Andrews 1953/56; Pfouts 1957; Massey 1973).

Quite contrary to the neoclassical theory, Myrdal (1957) in his *cumulative causation theory* stresses the initial disparities and the rigidity of the system, pointing out that under such conditions the free play of market forces is bound to lead to unbalanced regional growth because of backwash effects; for instance, labour will move to regions already far developed; capital will do the same, deserting regions with less chance of development. Thus, in the next period the latter regions will have become even less attractive. The author did not perceive merely negative effects, recognising indeed the 'positive' spread effect, that is, the spill-over of growth from central to less favoured regions. Hirschman (1958) believed the spread effects to be stronger than the backwash effects.

A lot of efforts have gone into analysing the causes of agglomeration or *spatial concentration*. Three causes are generally recognised: (1) economies of scale, (2) agglomeration effects, and (3) urbanisation effects. Economies of scale are inherent to the firm; agglomeration effects are the advantages to be gained from the joint location of linked productions (an idea that has been worked out in the attraction theory, see Klaassen 1967), and by urbanisation effects are understood general advantages from the joint use of services etc.

In backward regions, all these advantages are largely absent; the *growth-pole theory*, developed in the context of regional policy, pleads their deliberate creation in regions where they are absent or insufficiently developed (Perroux 1955; Boudeville 1972; Paelinck 1965; Hermansen *et al*. Lasuen 1969, etc.).

The whole body of literature referred to so far relates to developments within national states. When national states form *economic unions to achieve market integration*, the consequences for *regional development* can be very important. Giersch (1949) examined the relation between agglomeration economies and regional development in an integrated market area. By his theory, if inter-European trade is freed from tariffs and quotas, and factors are at liberty to move all over Europe, the result will be international, intra-European agglomeration, for integration will make a highly industrialised centre attractive to even more labour and capital. By contrast, peripheral regions will be put at a greater disadvantage than before; the peripheral regions of a country that itself is peripheral to the centre of the European Community will suffer the most, for they will become even more peripheral in respect of the new super centre. On the other hand, regions on inner frontiers may derive some benefit from the integration.

The same phenomena appear a fortiori in a *monetary union*. As a matter of fact, Giersch (1949) already argued that "The creation of a monetary union transforms balance-of-payment problems into regional problems"! If the participating countries vary widely in their initial stages of development, the effect of monetary integration is likely to be negative (Marquand 1973; Williamson 1976).

On the other hand, integration may work positively for the

regional equilibrium of an area like that of the European Community, if the growth effect it engenders for all regions surpasses any negative influence on specific regions. (The theoretical effects of integration on different types of region is described in more detail in Vanhove and Klaassen 1987).

The spread of productive activities across Europe plays an important part, and *location factors* therefore carry great weight in location theory. We shall not continue our discussion of location theory here, but rather refer to the extensive treatise on both regional development theory and location theory on the European level by Vanhove and Klaassen (1987).

Production factors are to some extent mobile in Europe, as is apparent from industrial movement. A fairly complete analysis (see Klaassen and Molle 1982) has proved this movement to have often gone toward more equality (spread effects). Migration, on the contrary, has often had backwash effects (Van Haselen and Molle 1981). The highly mobile production factor capital also supports the tendency towards greater concentration.

One mechanism behind that tendency works through the banks, which centralise the savings of 'poor', often 'peripheral', regions and use them to provide 'concentration' regions with capital, because there the projects with the best financial prospects by the mesostructure of multiplant and multinational corporations (Holland 1976, 1979). In the same vein, Friedmann (1979) sees inequality rise as a consequence of the disturbed balance between the functional and territorial bases of socio-economic changes. Prospects are better in concentration regions than elsewhere because they are nearer to the market, able to employ specialised manpower, etc.

Apart from the market mechanism, also impulses from the political system do not always favour backward regions either. Think, for instance, of the effects of the tendency towards national wage-setting, which has done away with the relative wage-cost advantage many regions used to have. On the other hand, welfare-state policies have contributed to greater regional equilibrium (Molle 1986).

The instances given of the dynamics of regional development, to which many others could be added, may suffice to illustrate the general nature of the regional problem.

As the above discussion shows, under some conditions the system tends towards less disparity, under others towards more. Because the system appears unable to achieve equilibrium, governments have stepped in.

ECONOMIC AND SOCIAL MOTIVES

Traditionally, *two reasons for intervention* by measures of regional policy are given. The first is that large groups of the population feel that inequality is socially inacceptable and morally unfair; it is known in the literature as the 'equity argument' for regional policy. The second, of a typically economic nature, is known in the literature as the 'efficiency argument', which states that the deficient regional distribution of some production factors, public goods, and economic activity, prevents the economy from drawing full profit from the potential available, so that total production is less than it could be if the inequalities were removed. The motives for a European regional policy are also of a mixed social and economic character.

The *economic argument* for a European regional policy was already debated at the Messina Conference, but took some time to be translated into concrete policy. Although the fathers of the EC were well aware of the regional problems (as is evident from the preamble of the Treaty of Rome, according to which the member states are "anxious to reduce the differences existing between the various regions and the backwardness of the less favoured regions"), and in spite of repeated warnings by academics (e.g. Giersch 1949) that European integration spelled problems for certain regions, the treaty of the European Economic Community made no provisions for a European regional policy in the proper sense. The creation of the Common Market and the development of a common foreign-trade policy deprived member states of the trade-policy instruments by which they had supported regionally concentrated industries. Exposed to foreign competition, the least efficient ones (such as the Wallonian coal mines) soon found themselves out of business. The problems were aggravated when the free movement of production factors was introduced, and capital and labour began to flow to the most developed regions, as was to be expected. Furthermore, with the progress of harmonisation, especially on the industrial and social planes, national instruments lost much of their implicit power to control regional developments. The gradual realisation of an Economic and Monetary Union (EMU) is curtailing even more the instruments available to national states; they are losing, for example, the authority to pursue a national exchange-rate policy (Williamson 1976).

The effects of integration on regional equilibrium may be both positive and negative. Much depends on the initial situation, the capacity of regions to adapt, the growth effects of integration on all regions, etc. (see, among others, Williamson 1976, Vanhove and Klaassen 1987, ch. 6). Measures of regional policy are necessary to compensate the negative effects of the initial (Customs Union) and progressive further (EMU) integration. Besides, the day-to-day functioning of the European Community needs the constant accompaniment of adequate measures of regional policy. Structural changes due to economic, technological, environmental and social developments continue to occur, demanding continuous adaptation. Without measures of regional policy to compensate the afflicted regions, the very functioning of the Community may be in jeopardy. What has happened to the steel industry is illuminative. The lack of alternative activities in 'steel regions', where substantial cutbacks in employment were necessary during the latest recession, has induced certain member states to give heavy support to the established industry, to which other member states responded by threatening to close the frontiers. Now that would mean a direct violation of the foundations of the Community (free market and international specialisation), jeopardising the whole European structure, on which the prosperity and welfare of European have largely come to depend.

Obviously there are ample reasons, not only on the national but also on the European level, to put forward the traditional 'economic-efficiency' argument in favour of a European regional policy. But the *equity argument* or social motive for regional policy also has a European dimension, inasmuch as a regional transfer of resources would be an act of solidarity of prosperous with less prosperous regions in Europe. The recent tendency of the European Community to emphasise social and human aspects along with purely economic ones also favours efforts to improve regional equilibrium by measures of regional policy on the European level.

The question suggests itself, however, how far such arguments carry weight in the European context, where up till now neither the social dimension (see, for instance, Vandamme 1986) nor the basis for an appeal to redistributive justice (Findlay 1982) seem to have developed much.

Traditionally the framework for claims to solidarity has been the national state, where people feel they belong to one social system; it would be interesting to see how far the idea of the EC has come to supplement that of the nation state. Some empirical evidence on that score has come available from a survey held by the Commission (CEC 1983). A first interesting result of that survey is that a large majoirty of respondents favoured social or moral argument for measures of interregional transfer over efficiency arguments. Indeed, in the entire EC there are nearly twice as many supporters of aid to regions most in need of it than supporters of aid to regions making the best use of it. Although there are wide variations among countries, the general picture is the same in all member states.

The second interesting aspect is how European solidarity among regions compares with solidarity among regions of the same state. The survey shows that while four out of five respondents accept to pay a fiscal contribution for aid to regions in their own country, only one in three feels the same about aid to regions in other EC countries. That, too, is true of all the countries of the Community, with relatively slight differences among them.

DIMENSIONS

Objectives of EC policy

Regional policy has gradually developed in the national framework of all countries of Western Europe. Dependent on the gravity of their regional problems and the prevailing socio-economic views, they started sooner or later, and more or less intensively, as is apparent both from the number of instruments used and from the vigour with which they were applied. Gradually, however, some pattern has become visible in the multiplicity of ideas elaborated with respect to the tools of regional policy in the member states of the European Community, and a degree of consensus is gradually crystallising out; so, a few characteristics can now be given.

About the *instruments of regional policy* most people have largely the same ideas. In all member states the instruments applied can be divided into (1) instruments addressed to people and (2) instruments addressed to industries. The former group, in practically all countries far less important than the latter, concerns mainly financial support to persons willing to move house. The important group of instruments applied to activities falls apart into financial benefits supposed to encourage investments in certain regions on the one and (loans, grants, etc.), and on the other a wide category of instruments facilitating location in certain regions. The latter instruments are almost invariably concerned with infrastructure (roads, ports, industrial sites, training of workers, public utilities, etc.[1]

A few words are due, moreover, about the *objectives* at which regional policy is aimed. Some time ago the OECD summed up the objectives which the countries of Western Europe try to realise through their regional policy (OECD 1970); as they have remained practically unchanged since, we shall briefly reproduce them here. The objectives are:

— "planning economic development and investment in accordance not only with the need to promote the overall progress of the national economy, but also with the diverse needs and potentialities of the different regions and with the geographical distribution of the population and manpower;

— reducing the imbalance between regions in the distribution of economic activity and in the levels of income, prosperity and welfare;

— maintaining and encouraging the social and cultural basis of the life of the regional populations including the preservation and best use of natural, cultural and amenity resources;

— planning the physical environment and infrastructure including housing, communication, and other forms of fixed capital in accordance with consistent and coherent national, interregional and regional aims and with the economic resources available."

The *objectives* of European regional policy have been formulated at many places in different ways. One of the most representative official statements (CEC 1977) defines the following two objectives:

— to diminish current regional problems as they occur both in the traditionally less developed regions and in regions involved in a process of industrial and agrarian transformation;
— to prevent new regional disparities that could result from structural changes in the world economy.

The obvious next question is what the EC has done to attain these objectives. Little enough at first, mainly because it was poorly equipped. As a matter of fact, in 1958 nobody had a clear idea of the size and nature of regional problems on the European level. As we have seen, the Community set out without sufficient authority in regional matters from the Rome Treaty, and only got that authority by a lengthy procedure. By constant diligence the Commission has gradually acquired the necessary instruments, and the regional element has become more and more prominent among the policy areas of the EC. Now the Community regional policy is conducted in cooperation with the member states; indeed EC regional policy is not a substitute for, but a complement to the regional policies carried out by the member states.

Four main areas of EC activity in regional policy are generally distinguished (CEC 1977; CEC 1985b):

— the acquisition of knowledge of the regional problems in the EC;
— co-ordination of the EC policies in other areas (for instance agriculture);
— co-ordination of the regional policies of member states;
— financial intervention to contribute to the development of certain regions.

We will discuss them in succession.

Assessing the regional problems

The European Community is struggling with vast regional problems.[2] They vary widely and give rise to different *types of problem region*. On the one hand are the regions that so far have developed hardly any manufacturing industry and services, being still largely oriented to agriculture; especially in southern member states, agriculture is often not very productive. On the other hand are the regions which played a leading role at a certain stage of economic changed. The former type of region is generally marked by a peripheral situation and a deficient infrastructure, in particular a meagre endowment with business services. The latter type is generally marked by inadequate infrastructure and serious problems in old industrial as well as residential areas. The labour-market situation also differs in the two types of region. While agricultural regions lack skilled labour and industrial and service traditions, the trouble with the old industrial regions is that their mostly highly specialised manpower is at odds with modern requirements.

Until a short time ago the feeling was that central urban areas were growing too fast and in too high a concentration, and therefore had to be kept in check. Lately, however, policy makers have become aware that these so-called congestion areas have lost their strong position and are now also struggling to adjust their economic and social structure to the new circumstances.[3]

The disparity in *income per head* is generally felt to be one of the most painful disparities among the European regions. It is indeed wide, the best favoured region in the European Community being now 10 times 'richer' than the poorest. The figure has increased much with the latest extension of the EC; in the EC9 it was 'only' 5 times. Map 1 gives an illustration.

Extending earlier work (Molle c.s. 1980), Van Haselen and

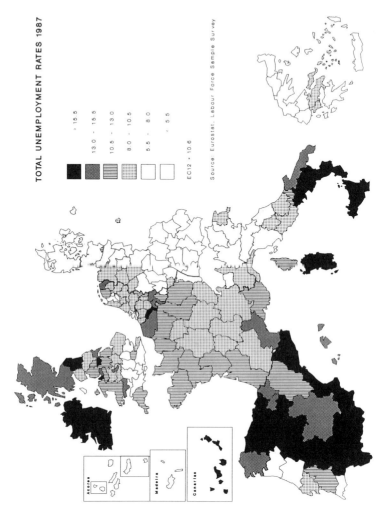

Map 1. Regional differences in GDP per head (*Source*: CEC, Third Periodic Report).

Molle (1987) have analysed the development of regional disparities in income with the help of the Theil index (see Table 1).

As the evolution of the figures in the first row shows, total

Table 1. Theil indices of Gross Regional Product by head of population in the EC, 1950, 1985.

	1950	1960	1970	1980	1985
1. Total disparity	0.124	0.102	0.078	0.098	0.071
2. Disparity among countries	0.095	0.081	0.061	0.082	0.056
3. 2:1 in %	76.4	79.2	78.7	83.5	79.3

Source: Van Haselen and Molle (1987).

disparity decreased considerably up to the first oil shock. The turbulent 1960s were attended by about an increase in the index, largely due, however, to differences between exchange rates and Purchasing Power Parities. Since 1977, disparity has again decreased. The second row gives the so-called between-sets, the disparity due to differences among countries. Row 3 clearly shows that international disparities are largely responsible for inter-regional disparities in Europe.

The causes of the decreasing disparity on the regional level are threefold.

First, movement of capital; indeed empirical studies in all European countries show that manufacturing plants have moved from central to peripheral areas (see Klaassen and Molle 1982). Second, the migration of workers (see Klaassen and Drewe 1973); contrary to that of capital, labour movement was rather centripetal. Third, and probably somewhat unexpected, the creation of the welfare state. As Molle (1986) has shown, the provision of such welfare services as schools, hospitals, transfer payments, and social-security systems have together strengthened the economic base of the less affluent regions.

Another indicator of regional disparity is *unemployment.* Although international comparison of the figures is difficult, Map 2 clearly shows that the highest unemployment rates are at

78

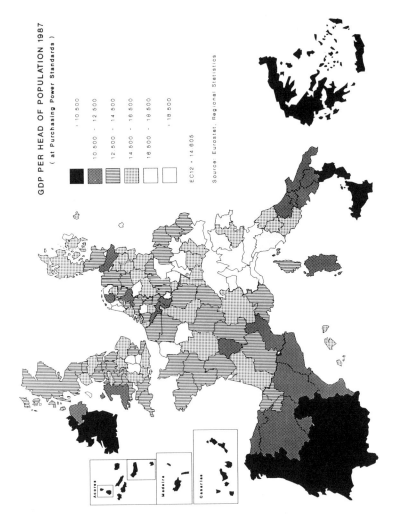

Map 2. Regional differences in unemployment (*Source*: CEC, Third Periodic Report).

present to be found in the Mediterranean basin, particularly in parts of Southern Italy and in almost all regions of Spain) and in the British Isles (especially in the Republics of Ireland and

Northern Ireland and some older industrialised regions of Great Britain).

The European ranking of prosperity evidences the remarkable *stability* of the position of individual regions. Indeed, through the 35-year study period, the 'peripheral' regions of Mediterranean countries were always in the lowest positions, while some urban, formerly 'congested' regions in northern Europe were steadily at the top. Only two significant shifts are recorded: all German regions moved strongly upward, and all regions of the United Kingdom fell back. Lately, the UK has once more shown a slight upward tendency.

Why is it that Mediterranean countries are so much inferior to northern Europe in income by head and unemployment, and why should the relative positions of the United Kingdom and Germany have changed? Both developments appear to be attributable to *national evolutions* and situations. The underlying factors, such as resources, the level of schooling of the labour force, the access to markets, and in particular the social and economic infrastructure, are national rather than regional characteristics. Therefore, to consider merely regional factors, as would be proper for regions within one single country, is not sufficient to cope with the regional problems within the EC; the so-called national factors should be given at least as much attention.

Co-ordination of EC policies with a regional impact

Specific policy measures have different effects on regions. That holds also for the EC. If, for instance, the tariff on textiles is reduced as a measure of common trade policy, textile activities that happen to be concentrated in a few regions may bear the brunt. That policies may have an adverse effect on regional equilibrium was made eminently clear by Henry (1981), who showed that the measures of agricultural policy, which consume three quarters of the EC budget, mainly benefit the rich regions. Woken up, the EC now tries to assess the probable regional impact of its other policies before implementing them.

Molle and Cappellin (1988) have tried to *establish the regional impact of the most important EC policies*. Given the complexities of the detailed studies on which they based their research (for instance trade, macro-economics, industry), only approximation proved possible. They have made a geographical division between north (N) and south (S) (based on the general welfare differences in Europe), and distinguished the usual four types of region: metropolitan, intermediate, agricultural/peripheral, and old industrialised. The scores of table 2 (+ for beneficial; 0 for neutral; — for negative; ? for unknown or indeterminate) indicate the shifts found in the detailed studies.[4]

Two major *conclusions* are warranted: (1) that Community policies tend to have contradictory effects, and (2) that the combined scores tend to accumulate more positive points to some regions (intermediate north) and negative points to others (in particular the problem regions of long standing in southern

Table 2. Schematic view of impacts by policy area and type of region.

Effect Policy area	Metropolitan		Intermediate		Agri/periph.		Old industrial	
	N	S	N	S	N	S	N	S
Agriculture	0	0	+	0	0	0	0	0
Industry	—	0	+	+	0	0	—	—
Energy	0	—	0	—	—	—	0	0
Transport/ Telecommunication	+	0	+	—	0	—	0	0
Social and Empl.	?	?	?	?	?	?	?	?
Trade	0	0	0	0	0	0	0	0
Macro and Monetary	+	0	+	0	0	—	0	0

Source: Molle and Cappellin (1988).

1 + beneficial 3 — negative
2 0 neutral ? unknown or indeterminate

Europe). Thus, the urgency attached by the EC to the analysis of policy impacts seems justified.

The response of European regional policy to the problems indicated has been inspired by the idea of compensation. That is hardly surprising, as in a sense the entire EC regional policy owes its existence to the UK claim to be compensated for losses due to integration. More specifically, European regional programmes like VALOREN (for energy), now being put into operation, try to compensate the regions in the very sector which has caused the the regional problem in the first place. For instance, if energy policy has aggravated a region's problem, a programme is drawn up to improve its energy situation. Molle and Cappellin (1988) favour an approach without that pronounced link, an approach by which regions are helped by all practical means to overcome their problems, whatever the cause. In such an 'endogenous' approach, the potential sources of conflict between Community, national and regional objectives and instruments seem to be far less virulent than in the compensation approach.

Co-ordination of member states' regional policies

All countries in western European have taken up regional policy in the course of the past decades. According to the gravity of their regional problems and the socio-economic views held, they started sooner or later, and more or less intensively, as is apparent both from the number of instruments used and from the vigour with which they were applied. Gradually, however, the multiple ideas on tools of regional policy developed in the member states of the European Community are setting in a kind of pattern, and some consensus is gradually crystallising out, so that now a few general characteristics can be given of regions and instruments.

If at first regional-policy efforts tended to focus almost universally on the so-called backward regions, or regions trying to adjust their structures, later on the conviction grew that the system of regions should be regarded as a whole, each element needing its own type of measure.

In all member states, the *instruments of regional policy* are now generally divided into (1) instruments addressed to people, and (2) instruments addressed to industries. The former category, which is practically everywhere less important than the latter, concerns mainly financial support to persons willing to move house. To·the important group of instruments applied to economic activities belong, first, financial benefits (loans, grants, etc.) meant to encourage investments in certain regions, and second, the large category of instruments encouraging location in certain regions. The latter instruments refer traditionally to infrastructure (roads, ports, industrial sites, training of workers, public utilities, etc.); recently, aspects of research and innovation have come to the fore.

If all governments are broadly agreed on the causes and remedies of regional problems, that does not mean they also take a European view. Actually, the national views tend to be distorted. What from a national point of view may seem a grave problem justifying a substantial money outlay, may seem trifling from the EC point of view. So, the first task of the EC was to define the *priority regions on the EC level*, that is, the regions that are eligible for aid from the European Regional Fund. Map 3 gives those so qualified in 1986.

The second task was to prevent governments from outbidding one another with subsidies, which would mean in practice that the richer member states would be able to match any package allowed to the poorer ones. The EC has put a *ceiling on aid levels* in each type of problem region, so that the effectiveness of a subsidy of, say, 50 percent in a very poor region should not be eroded by subsidies of 35 percent in relatively prosperous areas.[5]

Because the regional policy of the EC is complementary to that

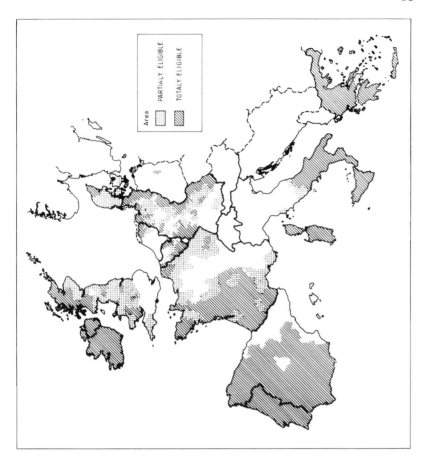

Map 3. Regions qualifying for aid from the ERDF (*Source*: CEC, Third Periodic Report).

of the member states measures need to be co-ordinated. Once that need had been recognised — as early as 1965 — a *regional programme* was drawn up and proposed as a policy instrument. It took almost 10 years to get that proposal accepted, but by now quite a number of policy programmes have been published.[6] Their purpose is to establish clearly what measures the competent organisations are taking in the regions involved with respect to infrastructure, schooling, housing, etc., so that the EC can co-ordinate them, identify any gaps, and design schemes to fill these up. Besides, the reports are to serve as a base for checking the progress of regional development.

For the smooth co-ordination of more general issues between the EC and the member states, and as a platform for regular discussions on priorities, programmes, and other matters, a *Committee for Regional Policy* has been installed, consisting of officials of the Commission and the national governments of the member states.

The European Regional Development Fund

For effective help to regions in distress, the EC must have financial means. After years of negotiation,[7] the EC finally obtained the necessary funds with the creation, in 1975, of the European Regional Development Fund.[8] The *tasks of the ERDF* are to grant subsidies to stimulate investment in economic activities and develop the infrastructure in specific regions designated as EC problem areas (see Map 3). Eligible for investment support are those activities which are already receiving aid from the member state in question or one of its agencies; the EC intervention is indeed meant to complement such aid. Apart from works directly related to manufacturing (industrial sites and such), more general infrastructure works, for instance the construction of roads and canals, also qualify for support. Member states are invited to submit projects, which are then compared with the 'regional programme' to evaluate their contribution to the solution of the region's problems. The Fund (approximately 12^9 Ecu for the 1975—1984 period) is fed by the EC budget, the Community's own means.

The *financial means of the Regional Fund are distributed in such a way as to strongly favour low-income countries.* Table 3 compares ERDF aid per capita to GDP per capita (in index figures). When interpreting the figure for Greece, keep in mind that Greece only started to benefit from the ERDF after 1981.

The enlargement of the EC with two low-income countries, the need to step up the efficiency of regional policy, and the introduction of other EC policies call for changes in the Fund and in other parts of EC regional policy. Two types of change were effected recently. First, the size of the Fund was increased, in 1987, to 3^9 M Ecu a year to cope with the increased range of regional problems. For a prompter response to new exigencies, the distribution of the funds among countries has been made more flexible. The shares are now as reproduced in Table 4.

The present distribution is stronger than the former oriented to low-income countries. Indeed, to make regional policy more effective, the amounts from the Regional Fund channelled to

Table 3. Concentration of ERDF aid (EC10), 1975—1984. (Indexes; EC = 100; aid per head and GDP per head)

Country	ERDF/P	GDP/P
Greece	261	40
Ireland	477	51
Italy	181	67
United Kingdom	116	90
France	74	117
Belgium	58	125
Denmark	28	115
Netherlands	25	116
Luxemburg	×	121
Germany	21	128
EC10	100	100

Source: Calculated from data in CEC 1985a.

Table 4. Minimum and maximum shares of countries in ERDF.

Country	Min	Max	Pivot
Belgium	0.6	0.8	0.7
Denmark	0.3	0.5	0.4
Germany	2.6	3.4	2.9
Greece	8.4	10.6	9.2
Spain	18.0	23.9	20.3
France	7.5	10.0	8.5
Ireland	3.8	4.6	4.1
Italy	21.6	28.8	24.5
Luxemburg	0.0	0.1	0.1
Netherlands	0.7	0.9	0.8
Portugal	10.6	14.2	12.1
United Kingdom	14.5	19.3	16.4
EC12	88.6	117.1	100.0

Source: Regulation EEC 3641.85.

long- standing problem areas have been stepped up. Such areas are usually found in countries with a structural GDP per head far below the EC average. Indeed, some 66 percent of the Fund (after enlargement, see Reg. EEC 3641.85; O.J. no. L.27.12.85) is now reserved to the four Mediterranean countries Greece, Italy, Spain and Portugal, which accommodate 36 percent of total population, but contribute only 22 percent of GDP to the EC 12.

The second change of the ERDF is a response to the *need for regional innovation*. The previous sections have described how the changes in the general economic and regional development of Europe after the crisis of the early 1970s, and its implications for regional policy, were accounted for. Regional policy used to rely very much on the mobility of industry, but now that the sources for that type of activity have dried up, every region falls back on its own indigenous potential. Moreover, regions have to be innovative, for standard solutions from outside are no longer forthcoming. Aware of the consequences, the European Commission submitted a proposal for a reoriented EC policy. Thereupon, the Council of Ministers adopted a new regulation of the Fund, introducing three new types of measure (Reg. EEC 1787/84 0.7.20.L 169, June 28, 1984). Measures of the first type are concerned with aid to companies in management and organisation questions, and allowances for the development of new products. The ERDF may also take measures to improve the infrastructure by stimulating the creation of agencies which compile and distribute information on product and process innovation. Finally, the ERDF may give support to companies by evaluating the technical feasibility and marketing prospects of new products and production processes. The main concern of the three types of measure is to assist small and medium-sized companies, which otherwise would have no access to such essential information.

EFFECTS

Effectiveness

Many authors have already posed the question how effective regional policy is, in other words, what the impact of certain instruments is. This question is part of a more extensive one, asking after the choice of goals, the generation of policy objectives etc. *Different theoretical views make for different approaches to policy.* Power theories (except the revolution Friedmann thinks necessary) imply that for regional policy to be effective, the government needs to take control of location decisions, for instance by nationalising key industries. That instrument, which has been effectively used in several member states (for instance Italy and France), cannot for the time being be wielded by the EC; it has to rely on 'influencing' rather than 'control' instruments.

All studies of the *effectiveness* of regional policy are hampered by the difficulty of relating a change in economic variables to the use of certain policy instruments. Attempts of various types have been made.

The simplest approach is to measure the effect of regional policy as the sum of all employment in activities that have been supported. It is an unsatisfactory approach, because it leaves unanswered the inevitable second question: how much of that employment would have been created anyhow, without regional support? To measure that quantity, *models* have been developed to isolate the effects of regional policy from 'normal' development. From such studies, regional policy seems to have only had limited effects.

Another apporach has been to *interview* the firms themselves, asking them how far their choice of location had been influenced by measures of regional aid. Again, the general conclusion was that current regional-policy measures cannot be hoped to affect the spatial distribution of economic activities in a big way (Uhrig 1983, Folmer 1986).

Welfare, satisfaction

In the previous sections we have seen that regional policy on the EC level has been pursued with increasing intensity. We have also seen that at least with respect to differences in wealth, measured in terms of regional income per head, there has been a decrease in disparity. However, that is a poor indicator of improvement, based as it is on a highly aggregate statistical concept. A more important fact to know would be whether the improved spatial distribution of income across Europe has increased welfare. Popular wisdom has it that more money does not make one happier. Some researchers say that more social help does not make people any happier either (Illich, 1971, 1977; Achterhuis, 1979). How to measure and compare the wealth and happiness of people is a problem that has been taken up by many economists, among them Easterlin (1974), Veenhoven (1984), and Scitovsky (1976). On the whole, scientific literature tends to uphold the popular wisdom referred to above. Because the subject is too complicated for an in-depth discussion at this place, we will content ourselves with analysing it with the help of a survey carried out by the Commission of the EC in the regions of the Community (CEC 1983). The objective was to find out how citizens appreciate the welfare position of their home region in relation to that of other regions.[9] Several criteria could be used to compare the subjective judgement of satisfaction with the equally subjective impression of regional prosperity. Employment opportunities appearing the dominant consideration, we have selected them as our principal indicator. The choice is justified, for the rankings of such variables as the region's relative situation with respect to specific sectoral development (agriculture, industry), income levels, transport infrastructure, prospects for young people, culture, services, etc., are all highly correlated with the 'good job opportunities' indicator.

In Table 5 we have grouped the regions into seven categories, from A to G, of different levels of economic health, as perceived by the people living in each region. The scores on 'good job opportunities' in the upper row show that in regions of type A, an

Table 5. Claims for support and degree of satisfaction of citizens in regions of various degrees of economic health. (Index: regions percentage in respect of EC9 percentage)

	A	B	C	D	E	F	G
Good job opportunities	133	130	109	108	88	70	65
Satisfaction	103	112	110	114	108	104	68

Figures based on data from EC 1983.

above-EC-average proportion of respondents judge their own region favourably; index 133, against index 65 in regions of type G. All respondents were asked whether they felt satisfied with the the life they were leading in the region. From the bottom row of Table 6 we see that the satisfaction felt by people in the seven types of region does not essentially correlate with their opinion of the region's general socio-economic situation. In six regional types, A to F, people showed themselves more or less satisfied, in the middle group (type D) even more so than in the richest (type A). That finding seems to confirm that more money or more social services do not make a man happier. Only in group G, the most deprived one, is satisfaction also far below average. But, as this group contains only Italian regions, national differences (see Table 6) may have had an influence.

To compare subjective measures such as satisfaction with more

Table 6. Wealth and satisfaction: national comparisons, 1981. (EC = 100)

	% share satisfied 1	GDP/P 2	% social security in GDP 3
Greece	76	46	—
Italy	88	69	92
France	92	118	101
Germany	104	120	110
Italy	109	56	91
UK	111	97	88
Belgium	112	108	113
Netherlands	121	110	118
Luxemburg	124	160	109
Denmark	125	125	109

Sources: 1. Eurobarometer 1981; 2 and 3. Eurostat: Review 1972—1981, Luxemburg 1983.

objective indicators of wealth would be interesting. Unfortunately, the lack of basic comparable data forbids such a comparison on the regional level. On the national level we do have the relevant data available. Table 6 gives information on satisfaction by country (column 1); the figures differ somewhat from those from the regional survey owing to conceptual differences. To these are added data on Gross Domestic Product by head (column 2) and the share of social security in total GDP (column 3). From a comparison of the column, satisfaction and income-by-head levels seem highly correlated, although some interesting national deviations can be observed. The correlation of satisfaction with the share of the welfare or social services is negligible. The degree of satisfaction has been followed for more than 10 years now; the figures reveal a remarkable stability through time; the ranking of the countries stays the same all through the period.

The crude analysis of subjective elements permits only the fairly general conclusion that the figures confirm the popular wisdom that more wealth, more employment, more money do not automatically make for higher satisfaction.

FINAL REMARKS

Outlook

In the near future, further steps will be taken on the path to complete integration. We refer here in particular to the proposed completion of the internal market (CIM) (see CEC 1985c) including the liberalisation of capital movements, and the further development of the European Monetary System (EMS). The former would lead to a more efficient allocation, the latter to stabler conditions, both conducive to economic growth.

The white paper of the Commission seeks to remove the

physical, fiscal and technical barriers between national markets within the EC. Hopefully, the allocation of resources within the Community will become more efficient as "resources both of people and materials, and of capital and investment" are encouraged to "flow into areas of greatest economic advantage". The paper shows awareness (Art. 15) that some possible results of the White Paper's implementation might deter individual member states from endorsing the proposals. Widening regional disparities could be one reason for holding back. In that way, the large positive effects which the CIM and EMS could have for all, might fail to be realised because certain small (net) negative effects for some were not compensated.

Are such adverse developments likely to occur and if so, what form will they take? In a recent study (CAM 1987), an attempt has been made to answer those questions. No empirical investigations having been made as yet, the answers can at best be tentative.

1. One effect is that the internal market will *increase* GDP and hence *demand*. How regions will benefit is difficult to say. Some, specialising in slow-growth activities, stand to lose, others, oriented to high-growth activities, stand to gain. Growth is therefore unlikely to spread evenly across all regions.

2. A second effect is the *relocation of activity due to increased specialisation* and the grasping of economies of scale. Where such concentration is going to occur is not clear. One would expect it to be in regions already showing great dynamism, but history has taught us that others may have as good a chance of development. For each specific activity, in the end the region's potential for gains and losses will be determined by the relative value of such location factors as market access, infrastructure, manpower qualification, etc. A general conclusion from the study of these factors is "that weaker regions must expect to lose economic activity in sectors which are opened up by the completion of the internal

market. The way this is likely to happen is different for different types of region:

— agricultural (often peripheral) regions may find it more difficult to overcome entry barriers, including distance barriers;
— because of their locational profile, areas of industrial decline are least likely to keep existing activities that need to be concentrated, or to attract newly created activities;
— prospering intermediate regions may find themselves increasingly vulnerable as the mass production in which they specialise is rationalised.

Finally, the completion of the internal market also implies that the market for *public procurement* is opened up. Producers of defense goods may continue to be protected for some time, but producers for public utilities, especially telecommunication and infrastructure, will be severely affected. They seem to be present in all types of region.

Conclusion and evaluation

In the previous section we have found that the regional *disparities* in the European Community (12 members) have gradually decreased, gainsaying the fears expressed by many that the implementation of Customs Union would reinforce the diverging tendencies in Europe and widen the disparities. We have also found that the spatial disparities in Europe were largely due to disparities between member states. Therefore, policy measures to diminish disparity among regions would have to concentrate on diminishing national differences.

An analysis to the *regional policy* pursued by the EC to remedy the unequal regional situation has revealed that it has gradually evolved from mere study through co-ordination to financial influencing. The main instruments are designed to get entrepreneurs to settle in problem areas, and to finance the construction of infrastructure meant to make these regions more attractive to investors. The effectiveness of these instruments has not yet been satisfactorily assessed.

Can regional policy *adequately solve the problems* in hand? Since they spring mostly from differences among member states, the use of regional-policy instruments may be questioned. Of course, the large sums channelled to poor member states through the ERDF are used for development purposes. More financial help is provided along other budget lines (such as the Agricultural and Social Funds), but the net transfer of money through the EC budget is not unquestionably benefiting the poorer member states. That conclusion does not seem to change much when invisible transfers are included.

So, the *conclusion* must be that, if the objectives are taken seriously, a more *comprehensive EC redistributional policy* has to be defined, including, besides regional and social policies, a mechanism for the transfer of considerable funds that can be used by the poorer members states for general structural growth policies.

To recognise the desirability of providing more means does not yet imply that they are in fact provided. Evidently, a much greater appeal will have to be made to European solidarity, a notion that so far has not been put in practice very much. On the contrary, member states, though co-operating in the Community, do so in free competition, every country trying to get the better of the others in the various negotiations. The whole decision-making mechanism of the European Community would have to be changed thoroughly to make it solidarity-oriented. That in times of economic slowdown the richer countries will be found willing to transfer large sums of money, is hard to imagine.

The increasing interplay of regional and national problems in the European Community may give rise to the question *whether regional policy in the strict sense is still necessary on the level of the Community* or had better be left to the member states themselves. The answer could be yes to the latter, if there were better alternative mechanisms to foster the equilibrium among member states. Because in practice that is not so, however, the limited instruments of EC regional policy, though perhaps not the most adequate, are still better than nothing. And even if there were such mechanisms, some form of European regional policy would still be desirable to check, on the European level, the spatial consequences of certain national and EC policy measures, and to compensate them as far as possible. That would be better than having the problems attacked afterwards by the member states. To the same extent that the EC wants to keep informed about the sectoral (or social, monetary, third-world) dimension of its policy, the spatial element needs to be represented in total EC policy.

NOTES

1. For a detailed survey of the instruments of both groups in force in each country in the past, Allen *et al.* (1979), and for a more recent survey, Yuill and Allen (1985).
2. For a good review, see CEC (1987). From the beginning, the Commission has been active in assessing the regional situation and regional developments in the Community by carrying out or commissioning several studies (CEC 1961, 1964, 1971, 1973). The main purpose of the reports is to keep up the knowledge of the old problems up-to-date and recognise new problems as soon as they present themselves. They also serve as a foundation for discussions with member states about priorities in regional policy and the changes to be carried through in it. Recently it was agreed that the Commission would periodically write reports on the regional situation in the Community (CEC 1981/84a/87).
3. See in this connection Klaassen, Molle and Paelinck (1981) and Van den Berg (1982).
4. For many of the detailed studies, quantitative results were either not available or their underlying concepts could not be made comparable. That is why we have to be content with these fairly crude indicators.

5. For a review of national instruments, see Yuill and Allen (1985).
6. CEC (1979) reviews the older programmes, CEC (1984b) the more recent ones.
7. Discussed at the Messina Conference back in 1956, proposed by the Commission in 1969.
8. For a description of the creation of the Fund, see Talbot (1977), and for a review of its performance in the first 10 years, see the EC brochure CEC (1985).
9. Note that nine out of ten respondents considered only other regions in their own country; only one in ten took other countries into account.

REFERENCES

Achterhuis, H. (1979), *De markt voor welzijn en geluk* (The market for welfare and happiness), Ambo, Baarn.
Allen, K., *et al.* (1979), "Regional Incentives in the European Community; a Comparative Study", EC Collection Studies, *Regional Policy Series* no. 15, Brussels.
Andrews, R. B. (1953/1956), "Mechanics of the Urban Economic Base", series of articles in *Land Economics*, vols. 29—31.
Berg, L. van den, R. Drewett, L. H. Klaassen, A. Rossi and C. Vijverberg (1982), *Urban Europe, a Study of Growth and Decline*, Pergamon Press, London.
Boudeville, J. R. (1972), *Aménagement du territoire et polarisation*, Génin, Paris.
CAM (1987) (Cambridge Economic Consultants), *Regional Impact of Policies Implemented in the Context of Completing the Communities' Internal Market by 1992*, Cambridge.
CEC (1961), *Document de la Conférence sur les économies régionales*, vol. II, Brussels.
CEC (1964), *Reports by Groups of Experts on Regional Policy in the European Economic Community*, Brussels.
CEC (1971), *Regional Development in the Community: Analytical Survey*, Brussels.
CEC (1973), *Report on the Regional Problems in the Enlarged Community* (Thomson Report), Com. 73/550, Brussels.
CEC (1977), "The Regional Policy of the Community, New Guidelines", *Supplement 2/77 to the Bulletin of the EC*.
CEC (1979), "The Regional Development Programmes", *Regional Policy Series*, no. 17, Brussels.

CEC (1981), *The Regions of Europe: First Periodic Report*, Brussels.

CEC (1983), *The Europeans and Their Regions*, Commission DG XVI, Internal Documentation.

CEC (1984a), *The Regions of Europe; Second Periodic Report on the Situation and Socio-economic Evolution of the Regions of the Community*, Brussels.

CEC (1984b), *Les programmes de développement régional de la deuxième génération pour la péiode 1981—1985*, Collection Documents, Bruxelles.

CEC (1985a), *The European Community and its Regions; 10 Years of Community Regional Policy and the ERDF*, Luxemburg.

CEC (1985b), *Main Texts Governing the Regional Policy of the EC*, Collection Documents, Brussels.

CEC (1985c), *Completion of the Internal Market* ('White Paper'), Com (85)310, Brussels.

CEC (1987), *Regional Disparities and the Tasks of Regional Policy in the Enlarged Community (Third Periodic Report)*, Brussels.

Easterlin, R. A. (1974), "Does Economic Growth improve the Human Lot? Some empirical evidence", in P. A. David and M. W. Ruder (eds), *Nations and Households in Economic Growth*, Academic Press, New York/London.

Folmer, H. (1986), *Regional Economic Policy*, Nijhoff, Dordrecht.

Friedmann, J. (1979), "On the Contradictions between City and Countryside", in H. Folmer and J. Oosterhaven (eds), *Spatial Irregularities and Regional Development*, Nijhoff, Boston.

Giersch, H. (1949), "Economic Union between Nations and the Location of Industries", *Review of Economic Studies*, vol. 17, pp. 87—97.

Hagenaars, A. J. M. (1986), *The Perception of Poverty*, North Holland, Amsterdam.

Haselen, H. van, and W. T. M. Molle (1981), "Regional Patterns of Natural Population Growth and Migration in the EC of Twelve", *NEI/FEER*, 1981/12, Rotterdam.

Haselen, H. van, and W. Molle (1987), *Regional Economic Policy*, Nijhoff, Dordrecht.

Haselen, H. van, and W. Molle (1987), "Divergence or Convergence between the Centre and, Periphery of Europe; an Analysis of the Very-Long-Term Trends", *NEI/FEER* 1987/22.

Henry, P. (1981), *Study of the Regional Impact of the Common Agricultural Policy*, Luxemburg.

Hermansen, T., *et al.* (1970), *A Review of the Concepts and Theories of Growth Poles and Growth Centers*, UN Research Institute for Social Development, Geneva.

Hirschmann, A. O. (1958), *The Strategy of Economic Development*, Yale University Press, New Haven, Conn.

Holland, S. (1976), *Capital versus the Regions*, MacMillan, London.

Holland, S. (1977), "Capital Labour and the Regions", in H. Folmer and J. Oosterhaven (eds), *Spatial Inequalities and Regional Development*, Nijhoff, Boston.

Illich, I. (1971), *Deschooling Society*, Harper, New York.

Illich I., *et al.* (1977), *Disabling Professions*, Boyers, London.

Kaldor, N. (1966), *The Causes of the Slow Growth of the United Kingdom*, Cambridge University Press, Cambridge.

Klaassen, L. H. (1967), *Methods of Selecting Industries for Depressed Areas*, OECD, Paris.

Klaassen, L. H., W. T. M. Molle and J. H. P. Paelink (eds) (1981), *Dynamics of Urban Development*, Gower, Farnborough.

Klaassen, L. H., and P. Drewe (1973), *Migration Policy in Europe*, Saxon House, Farnborough.

Klaassen, L. H., and W. T. M. Molle (eds) (1982), *Industrial Migration and Mobility in the European Community*, Gower Press, Aldershot.

Lasuén, J. R. (1969), "On Growth Poles", *Urban Studies*, vol. 6, pp. 137—161.

Marquand, I. (1973), "The Basic-Service Categorisation in Planning", *Regional Studies*, vol. 7, pp. 1—15.

Molle, W. (1980), with the assistance of B. van Holst and H. Smit, *Regional Disparity and Economic Development in the European Community*, Saxon House, Farnborough.

Molle, W. T. M. (1983), "Technological Change and Regional Development in Europe (Theory, Empirics, Policy)", *Papers and Proceedings of the Regional Science Association European Coungress*, pp. 23—38.

Molle, W. T. M. (1986), "Regional Impact of Welfare State Policies in the European Community", in J. H. P. Paelinck (ed), *Human Behaviour in Geographical Space*, Gower Press, Aldershot.

Molle, W., and R. Cappellin (1988), *Regional Impact of Community Policiesin Europe*, Avebury/Gower, Aldershot.

Myrdal, G. (1957), *Economic Theory and Underdeveloped Regions*, Duckworth, London.

OECD (1970), *The Regional Factor in Economic Development, Policxies in Fifteen Industrialised OECD countries*, OECD, Paris.

Paelinck, J. H. P. (1965), "La thérie du développement régional polarisé", *Cahiers de l'ISEA* (Série L, no. 15, Economies Régionales), pp. 5—47.

Paelinck, J. H, P., and P. Nijkamp (1976), *Operational Theory and Method in Regional Economics*, Saxon House, Farnborough and Lexington, Mass.

Perroux, F. (1955), "Note sur la notion pôle de croissance", *Economie Appliquée*, vol. 8, pp. 307—320.

Pfouts, R. W. (1957), "An Empirical Testing of the Economic Base Theory", *Journal of the American Institute of Planners*, vol. 23, no. 2.

Pinder, D. (1983), *Regional Economic Development and Policy; Theory and practice in the EC*, G. Allen & Unwin, London.

Pollard, S. (1981), *Peaceful Conquest, the Industrialisation of Europe 1760— 1970*, Oxford University Press, Oxford.

Richardson, H. W. (1973), *Regional Growth Theory*, MacMillan, London.

Scitovski, T. (1976), *The Joyless Economy*, Oxford University Press, Oxford.

Talbot, R. B. (1977), "The European Community's Regional Fund 1977", *Progress in Planning*, vol. 8, part 3, pp. 183—281.

Uhrig, R. (1983), *Pour une nouvelle politique de développement régional en Europe*, Economica, Paris.

Vandamme, J. (ed) (1985), *New Dimensions in European Social Policy*, TEPSA, Croom Helm, London.

Vanhove, N., and L. H. Klaassen (1987), *Regional Policy, a European Approach* (2nd edition), Gower, Aldershot.

Veenhoven, R. (ed) (1984), *Betere wereld, gelukkiger mensen?* (Better world, happier people?), Swets & Zeitlinger, Lisse.

Williamson, J. (1976), "The Implication of European Monetary Integration for the Peripheral Areas", in J. Vaizey (cd), *Economic Sovereignty and Regional Policy*, Gill and Macmillan, Dublin.

Yuill, D., and K. Allen (eds) (1985), European Regional Incentives, CSPP University of Glasgow.

Energy policy

DAVID HAWDON

1. INTRODUCTION

The new Community Energy Policy Objectives for 1995[1] approved
by the Council of Ministers in September 1986 represent the
latest in a series of attempts to establish a co-ordinated energy
policy amongst the member states. Such attempts have from the
outset faced considerable difficulties. In the first place, unlike
agriculture no mention is made of energy in the Treaty of Rome
establishing the Community. Thus the Commission has had difficulty in winning acceptance of the need for a coordinated policy
amongst the member countries. Secondly the energy situations of
the member countries have little in common — some are significant energy importers (see Table 1), others are producers as well
as consumers and all have different traditions of government
intervention in the operation of the energy sector and in levels of
public subsidy. The Commission has had more success in achieving agreement to resolutions on principles than in obtaining decisions. In addition the formal consultative procedure within the
Community is responsible for substantial delays in the adoption
of proposals. For example, the latest energy policy decisions were
based on Commission proposals put forward in mid 1985 which
in turn arose out of analyses made in 1984. It is the purpose of

P. Coffey (ed.), Main Economic Policy Areas of the EEC – Toward 1992. pp. 101–123.
© 1990 Kluwer Academic Publishers, Dordrecht – Printed in the Netherlands.

Table 1. Net energy imports as a percentage of gross inland energy consumption.

	1973	1979	1984	1985
Eur 10	64.3	55.1	43.6	41.3
(Eur 12)				43.3
Belgium	88.0	88.0	70.9	69.9
Denmark	99.6	97.9	85.1	81.5
Germany	55.7	57.3	49.3	50.1
Greece	91.4	82.3	64.5	63.0
France	81.7	81.4	60.7	57.1
Ireland	85.7	83.6	57.5	60.6
Italy	85.7	83.6	85.0	84.1
Luxemburg	99.8	99.5	98.9	99.5
Netherlands	22.9	4.8	10.7	6.2
United Kingdom	50.2	12.0	−11.3	−15.5
Portugal				91.9
Spain				63.0

Background data on inland energy consumption and production (mtoe).

	1973	1979	1984	1985
Energy Consumption				
Eur 10	930.2	986.3	912.1	948.3
(Eur 12)			990.9	1029.2
Energy Production				
Eur 10 Prodn.	344.6	455.1	507.6	560.7
of which U.K.	110.1	192.6	203.8	233.7
Non-U.K.	234.5	262.5	303.3	327.0
(Eur 12)			533.5	888.6
Net Imports				
Eur 10				
of which U.K.	620.3	558.7	406.7	399.4
Non-U.K.	113.1	27.9	−21.9	−30.8
(Eur 12)			483.7	482.5

Source: Eurostat.

this paper to consider the development of energy policy in Europe in relation to relevant economic criteria for policy making and then to try briefly to evaluate the policy's success and to indicate some directions for future policy making.

2. ECONOMIC ANALYSIS OF ENERGY POLICY

Any kind of economic policy, including energy policy must contain three elements — goals or objectives, operational targets derived from them, and policy measures or instruments by which the specific targets are to be achieved. Out of the many alternative policies which may be available some selection has to be made. To what extent is it possible to evaluate the results of this policy selection process? We may do so in terms of the usual criteria of economic efficiency and distributive justice as well as of certain factors specific to the energy market.

Economic efficiency is concerned with two aspects technical or managerial efficiency and allocative efficiency. The former has to do with the relationship between inputs and output. For example, for any given level of inputs of coal, gas or oil, have we achieved maximum output levels of generated electricity? If not there is technical inefficiency. Similarly, if for any given level of output we could save on the use of any or all inputs we would not be attaining an efficient outcome perhaps due to managerial incompetence or ignorance. This type of efficiency is a necessary but not sufficient condition for allocative efficiency. Clearly there could well be many "state of the art" methods of producing electricity, each one having its own technically efficient production arrangements. Allocative efficiency is obtained by choosing the production method for which the sum of the input costs is minimum for a given level of output or, equivalently, which maximises output for a given level of costs. Behind this lies the idea that scarce resources are only allocated efficiently if it is impossible by varying inputs and outputs (i.e. changing resource allocation) to make someone better off in the economy without making others worse off.

Under ideal conditions such allocative efficiency could be achieved by perfectly competitive markets functioning without government intervention. In reality and in the energy markets in particular, market imperfections abound. The world price of oil is affected by the OPEC grouping of oil producer nations which, although not until recently a formal cartel with market sharing arrangements, has undoubtedly maintained cohesion among its members and inhibited downward pressures on prices. Again many energy utilities, especially in Europe, are owned or controlled by government agencies and possess varying degrees of monopoly power. Government intervention in energy pricing and investment can in principle alter the market outcomes from those which we should expect from the existence of the imperfections described e.g. higher prices, higher profit returns, lower factor payments and lower output levels. There is however potential (and frequently actual) conflict between such concerns and the need to motivate management and ensure the financial viability of energy enterprises by establishing minimum target rates of return or profitability objectives.

The cost and availability of energy clearly also has distributional aspects. Thus governments are likely to be concerned about the effect of policy on the distribution of real income among households. Energy may be subsidised for various specific groups deemed to be in especial need either by specific subsidy or through general social security provision as in the U.K.

Two further micro economic impacts should also be considered. In the first place any subsidy policy involves not only income transfers but also impacts on the level of employment since output will be larger than otherwise. Secondly the authorities may not be so much concerned about levels of income but about the magnitude of shocks to various groups in society. Thus windfall profits have been of more concern than gradual effects on income distribution (see Schmallensee[2]) and policy will vary accordingly.

Apart from these micro economic issues, policy is likely to take into account such macro economic impacts as the effects of rising energy prices on inflation rates, international trade between energy rich and energy deficient countries, and the overall level of "risk" to which the economy is exposed. Thus undue dependence on imported oil, it is often argued, increases the risk that the country may suffer severely if supplies are varied by the exporters. The cost of this risk can be measured in terms of the amounts of GDP which would be sacrificed through sudden reductions in energy input availability. One estimate for the U.S. (2) has put the expected cost of shortage at around $3 per barrel. The problems of computing any such cost are, however, quite formidable. They require an assumption that domestic supplies are inherently less risky and that is at least questionable in the light of recent U.K. experience in regard to domestically produced coal. Nevertheless arguments have been put forward for an oil import tax to indicate to the resource user that the fuel he consumes has associated security costs. These costs can be offset to some extent by storage of oil which in principle should proceed to the point where the marginal cost of storage equals the marginal expected risk premium on imports.

3. THE DEVELOPMENT OF EUROPEAN ENERGY POLICY

For the legitimisation of its role in the energy policy area, the European Commission looks back to meetings of the Heads of State of the Community members in Paris in 1972 and in Copenhagen in 1973. In 1972, the Commission was instructed to prepare the basis for a coordinated energy policy. Interestingly they put forward two scenarios — one of which was that oil prices would remain low and the other that oil prices would remain low and the other that oil prices would increase substantially. When in 1973 this second scenario was borne out, the Heads of State at their Copenhagen meeting (December 1973) turned to the Commission for more specific recommendations. These early days saw energy policy conceived in crisis, almost strangled at birth and thereafter exhibiting all the symptoms of a battered babyhood — apparent neglect by the Council and the recipient of well meaning but ineffective criticism of outsiders. The Council rejected the Commission's first response but eventually passed a resolution endorsing a revised policy document[3] which remained official Community policy until overtaken by events in 1979. A summary of the 1974, 1980 and 1985 policies is given in Table 2.

Behind the detail of the policy document it is possible to discern a number of underlying real objectives. In the first place there was concern for *security* of energy supplies.[4] The 1973 crisis was seen as a threat to the availability of a basic factor of production without which economic growth would cease or at least be severely constrained. There is implicit an assumption of a clear link between energy input and economic output and a perception of the inadequancy of the market mechanism to promote substitution of alternative energy sources for oil without some form of intervention. The question of the value of greater security and the costs of insecurity were not discussed so that the individual measures designed to improve security are difficult to assess. Since no effort was made to place a price on security, the possibility of an import tax designed to improve security was not considered, and instead the Commission recommended all sorts of targets for reducing oil (and especially oil import) dependence, and increasing the availability of substitute energy sources (see Table 2).

The second concern was with *stability* of energy prices. Prices

Table 2. Energy objectives of the European community.

Policy Target year	1974 1985	1980 1990	1986 1995
Import *dependence*			
Energy	50% (40% if poss)		
Oil	38% (28%) total energy	Less than 33.3% energy	
Energy *consumptn.*			
Energy	15% reduction		
Elect	35% of energy		
Oil		40% of total energy cons.	40% of energy consumption
Energy *supply*			
Prodn			
Oil	180 mtoe		
Solid	180 mtoe		Increase[1] share
Brown & Lignite	30 mtoe		
N. Gas	175—225 mtoe	Maintain share	
Nuclear	160—200 Gwe capacity		
Hydro+ Geo	45 mtoe		
New+ Renew			Substantial increase[2]
Imports			
Oil	540 mtoe		
Coal	40 mtoe		
R D&D	Yes	Yes	Yes

Table 2 (Continued)

Policy	1974	1980	1986
Target year	1985	1990	1995

Energy efficiency		PE/GDP growth ratio < 0.7	FD/GNP ratio reduce by 20%[3]
Electricity input mix		Coal + Nuclear = 70—75% of inputs 15%	Oil + Gas less than 15%[4]
Energy pricing		Yes	Yes

Resolution 17/12/74. OJC 153 1975	18/6/80. OJC 149 1980	16/9/86 OJC 241 1986. Proposal COM 245 (85).

Note: PE Primary Energy, FD Final Demand.
1. Original proposal was to "maintain and if possible increase" solids production. Com. 245 (85).
2. Commission proposed a 3 fold increase in new and renewables.
3. Original proposal was for a 25% reduction. Com. 245 (85).
4. Original proposal was for oil plus gas contribution of not more than 10%. Also the Commission proposed that the share of nuclear should be 40%.

were not seen as reflecting and signalling changes in the scarcity of resources, rather they were perceived as imposing costs on investment decision makers, making it more difficult for them to justify long term investments in alternative energy sources and thereby reducing the effectiveness of any energy policy requiring such investments. There seems to have been a presumption that firms in the energy supply industry were not able to evaluate risks and make the necessary adjustment to required rates of return before engaging in investment. And yet it is not clear why investors having discounted the likely risks should not undertake projects with positive expected cash flows in the energy area to the same degree as in any other sector. Any programme of accelerated investment in the face of market risk must increase rather than diminish risk and increase costs to society. One thing is clear, the Commission's arguments were not based on either of the traditional economic arguments for intervention — to improve market efficiency or to prevent substantial income redistribution.

Thirdly, there is a concern for the impact of higher oil prices on the *balance of payments* of what was a largely importing group of countries. This was seen rather vaguely as a cost of holding external debt in order to maintain the same value of imports. In such circumstances it is clear that heavily import dependent countries must either increase their foreign indebtedness, reduce internal demand or allow currency depreciation to cope with changes in balances of payments. But it is not clear that coordinated action at a Community level would lead to a better outcome than might be expected were each country to act in its own interests according to the balance of its disequilibrium and adjustment costs.

Finally there was the desire for a *harmonised* Common Market approach to the energy crisis. There was a concern that the different circumstances of the individual member countries would lead to "divergence in policies and priorities" and in consequence "wipe out the potential advantages of a unified common market". In contrast the potential benefits of harmonisation were seen to lie in an opportunity to spread risks — a kind of insurance argument.

From these basic preferences, the individual policies advocated by the Commission readily followed — a greater dependence on nuclear energy to promote supply security and satisfy a more flexible consumer demand for electricity; a heightened use of gas to satisfy current environmental anxieties and to provide a pipe-work network suitable for the eventual transmission of substitute gas alternatives, and a substantial R & D programme to overcome technical difficulties facing the development of less oily technologies for the longer term future. Sixteen specific targets were set by the Commission for the year 1985 (see Table 2), amongst which the most important were that import dependence was to be reduced to 40% (from 63% in 1973) while the share of oil in total energy supply was to be reduced to 38% (from 60% in 1973).

It was claimed that these targets were not arbitrary but were based on a consideration of relevant macroeconomic objectives (in particular a 4.5% p.a. economic growth rate), and of energy constraints. Most of these constraints seem designed to show why oil dependence could not be reduced further than 40%, for example the claim that substitution between fuels in demand was difficult, that there were commitments to support existing energy forms (e.g. coal) and that the outcome of long term investments in energy supply was uncertain. More to the point however, the Commission was vague on policy instruments — mentioning but not quantifying an oil tax option and elaborating only on Community expenditures designed to promote long term energy investments. However, R & D expenditure is notoriously unpredictable in its effect, the most important of which may be extremely long term. Again bureaucrats are likely to make arbitrary judgments on the prospects for research programmes and these may increase the risks of misallocation of funds. Thus we have a problem of lack of policy instruments — too few in relation to the objectives — contrary to an elementary result of the theory of economic policy.[5] Finally it was based on the rather naive assumption that the members would sacrifice their own interest in order to harmonize policies. Instead they vigorously promoted their own conflicting energy interests e.g. those of the coal industry in the U.K. and those of coal consumers and importers in Italy and so effectively prevented the adoption of the Commission's proposals for coal.

4. THE SECOND PHASE 1979–1985

In 1978/79, the constraints facing energy policy makers in Europe were suddenly tightened by the interruptions to oil supplies occasioned by the onset of the Iran/Iraq war. This however merely aggravated a situation of sharply increased world oil prices and greater than expected rates of energy demand in a period of relatively high economic growth. These events were taken by the Commission to illustrate Europe's extreme vulnerability to exogenous shocks in energy abailability and to justify the call for fresh and more effective energy policies. The main features of the new policy which emerged as the Council Resolution of 18th June 1979[6] were firstly a realisation of the unreality of certain of the 1974 objectives e.g. on oil import limitations, secondly an emphasis on the role of coal especially in electicity generating, so that nuclear power would not need to bear all the responsibility for displacing oil in this sector and thirdly a tightening of the energy consumption objective. The main innovation in the new policy was that the targets were now expressed in terms of ratios of growth in energy consumption to GDP growth rather than merely in terms of absolute consumption levels. For the rest the policy simply repeated, although in much less detail, the 1974 objectives but now extended forward to 1990 in place of 1985. The overriding importance of security of supplies was still emphasized on the basis of an argument that the costs of being out of stock were substantially greater than those of having an excess supply of an equivalent amount.[7] The Commission made no attempt to qualify their objectives, even though the member states indicated substantial margins of uncertainty particularly in their forecasts of natural gas, nuclear availability and energy conservation.

Much of the 1979/80 policy emphasis on speeding up energy savings and stimulating coal production stems from a conviction that the mid 1980's would witness renewed pressure on energy supplies as non OPEC oil sources began to contract. The price rises of 1978 were taken to indicate that adjustment times available were shorter than had been anticipated. What the Commission failed to appreciate was the cumulative impact of both 1973 and 1978 price movements on the level of energy demand — both through structural changes away from energy intensive activities and through substitution effects — which were already removing the need for massive supply expansion.

5. THE THIRD PHASE: 1985 ONWARDS

By 1984, the Commission itself conceded that many of its targets (for 1990) were now no longer relevant.[8] The Commission argued that the majority had been achieved early, that this showed the effectiveness of the 1980 policy, that however there was a danger of complacency and that new policies for the medium and long term were needed. It is clear however that the most significant changes in the European energy situation had occurred without Community involvement. On the supply side the rapid exploitation of North Sea gas had by 1983 reduced import dependence by almost 30%. Again the availability of natural gas imports from the Soviet Union had allowed a significant expansion of the share of gas in total energy supplies. The expansion of coal and nuclear power, heavily promoted by the Community, had on the other hand been much less than anticipated. On the demand side, energy efficiency whether measured in terms of primary energy or of final demand had improved much more significantly than envisaged by the Commission, and all sectors except transport witnessed an absolute decline in consumption between 1973 and 1982.[9] Finally, the balance of payments "constraint" was very much less than expected. By 1983 the cost of net oil imports into the EC (apart from France) was etimated by the IEA[10] to have fallen from \$70.2 billion in 1980 to \$41.9 billion in 1983 due to a combination of falling oil prices and reduced oil demand, neither of which had been anticipated by the Commission.

It may therefore seem somewhat surprising that the Commission advocated in its 1985 policy proposals further increases in energy efficiency of 25% by 1995, further reductions in the share of oil imports in total energy consumption, the maintenance of natural gas and coal market shares, an increased role for nuclear power and a tripling of the contributions from new and renewable energy sources. In order to justify this policy the Commission pointed to three types of risk to which European energy supplies had become vulnerable — the growing competitive demands of third world countries for energy supplies, the narrow margins which continue to exist between supply and demand in Europe and finally uncertainties about energy efficiency trends when prices are falling. It is not clear however why the extra demands from the third world should necessitate policy actions — they may simply reflect the fact that the more energy intensive activities as for example refineries and petrochemicals are diverting to these locations in response to comparative advantage factors. If the marginal productivity of energy is greater outside of Europe then, on efficiency grounds, everyone is potentially better off by a reallocation of energy resources away from Europe, and actually better off if trade restrictions are removed. The harmful social effects of the closure of energy inefficient industries might be dealt with better through general social security provision than through special energy policies. The other two arguments indicate that there remains a positive social cost associated with import dependence. This cost is essentially a shortage premium and might be expected to vary with such factors as capacity utilisation and political threats of major supply disruption. In the 1984/85 period when the new policy was being formulated, oil prices were falling as OPEC expanded production and there was little perceived threat of disruption. Under these circumstances it might have been expected that import dependency targets would have been relaxed. The policy implication is that import dependency targets ought to be more responsive to expected shortage penalities.

The actual objectives adopted by the Council in September 1986 show that not all of the Commission's arguments were accepted in their entirety. In particular less stringent targets were set for renewables development, reductions in energy intensity and in the share of hydrocarbons in electricity generation. These together with an increased role for solid fuels seem designed to make up for the abandonment of the Commission's ambitious target for nuclear development. Presumably the political costs of nuclear power post Chernobyl were considered to be too high for the Council to advocate precise goals in this area.[11]

6. THE SUCCESS OF POLICY

We may dispose of one popular criticism of European energy policy at the outset — namely that since the budgetary resources devoted to energy policy are small, significant effects cannot be expected. It is not the absolute size of the resources however but their size in relation to the incentive needed to change behaviour which is important. This may be quite small for simple conservation projects where the present value of projected cashflows is close to zero. Where projects are longer term and the risk premium is high, however, the incentive must be greater, and lack of budgetary resources may have more significant consequences.

"Success" may be judged in two ways — firstly in relation to the declared objectives of policy and secondly in relation to its general economic effects in terms of efficiency and equity.

Although it may be very difficult to assess whether broad objectives have been realised it is possible to test the detailed targets which the Commission has derived from its objectives. It is indeed rather surprising that the Commission should have been so explicit about its targets, although the availability of scapegoats in the form of national governments suggests that the incentive to fudge objectives may not have been great here. In any case, as Table 3 shows, the Commission's 1974 targets set for 1985 came nowhere near to being achieved. Gross energy consumption was overestimated by 33%, indigenous production by 30% and net imports by 38%. The most outstanding failures were in regard to oil consumption, net imports, and nuclear electricity generation and the targetted increase in new and renewable energy contribution did not occur. On the other hand, the Commission was not alone in making projection errors on quantities and it did rather better in terms of its share targets. Here its projections of net import dependency were almost fulfilled and the oil import ratio target was over-fulfilled. Nevertheless the Commission had been far too optimistic about the role of nuclear and in particular had not perceived the political and economic risks in the rapid exploitation of nuclear power.

Granted that the Community did not achieve its absolute targets it may be that the Community's policies made the member countries better off than they otherwise would have been. We will examine three areas — import dependency, energy intensity in relation to gross domestic product and price harmonisation. One way of testing whether belonging to the Community made any difference as regards import dependence across a wide variety of countries to membership of the Community. This procedure allows for the common policies pursued by wider groupings e.g. the IEA which might also have been expected to reduce import dependence. In fact the IEA grouping is a useful 'universe' since its members are relatively homogeneous in terms of economic

Table 3. European energy policy 1974: objectives and achievements (mtoe).

	1973 Actual	1985 Objective	1985[1] Actual	% Difference
Gross Energy				%
Consumption	973	1450	966	−33.4
Solid Fuels	222	250	218	−12.8
Oil (inc Bunker)	593	695	436	−37.3
Gas	118	270	182	−32.4
Primary				
Electricity	14	190	116	−39.0
Other	27	45	12	−73.3
Indigenous Products	365	800	562	−29.8
Solid Fuels	200	210	158	−24.8
Oil	12	180	149	−17.2
Natural Gas	114	175	127	−27.4
Nuclear	14	190	116	−39.0
Others	25	45	12	−73.3
Net Imports	613	650	403	−38.0
Solids	19	40	56	+40.0
Oil	589	515	286	−44.5
Natural Gas	3	95	59	−37.9
Electricity	—	—	1	—
Other	2	—	—	—
Ratios				
Net Import/GEC	63%	40%	42%	+2
Oil Share in Supply	60%	40%	45%	+5
Oil Imports/Oil ″	98%	75%	66%	−9
Solid share in ″	23%	>15%	22%	—
N. Gas share in ″	2%	25%	19%	−6
Nuclear/Electricity				
Supply	#%	50%	30%	−18

1. Energy in Europe No. 7. July 1987. European Communities.
NB. Differences between consumption and the sum of indigenous production and net imports are due to stock and bunker changes.

structure. The hypothesis that the EEC has had a significant impact on import dependence can be tested by estimating the regression relationship between import dependence and a dummy variable representing membership of the Community. Using IEA data for the period 1973 to 1983,[12] I estimated a linear relationship by O.L.S. between the rate of growth of the oil import share of total primary energy requirements (y^1) of each IEA member country) and membership of the EEC (EEC). The IEA data of course excludes France, and both the UK and Norway were also excluded since they are important oil producers and exporters.[12] The following results were obtained.

$$y1 = -2.9636 - 0.5239 \text{ EEC} \quad R^2 = 0.015$$
$$(-4.4422)(0.5095)$$

n = 19 (omitting Norway $\overline{R}^2 = 0.043$
              and the United
              Kingdom and excluding France)
     t-ratios in parenthesis.

These results give a very poor fit to the data. They do not support the hypothesis that membership of the Community significantly affected dependence on oil imports in the period. Including the U.K. and Norway has the effect of reducing the magnitude of the EEC effect but does not improve its significance. No significant improvement was made to the estimate either by allowing for economic growth (see Table 4).

Much of the Community's efforts to improve energy intensity were through measures designed to encourage investment in energy saving capital. A test of effectiveness is obtained by reexamining the relationship between Primary Energy/GDP ratios for the IEA countries. However here the ratios might well also be affected by regional factors (similarities of climate, culture, etc.)

Table 4. OLS analysis of EEC impact on oil import shares and energy intensity.

Dependent Variable	Independent Variables				R^2	$\bar{R}^2$	F	SE
	C	EEC	EUR	AGR				
Growth in Oil Import Share y^1	−2.9636 (−4.4422)	−0.5239 (0.5095)			0.015	−0.043	0.2596	2.2127
	−4.0551 (2.9718)	−0.2930 (−0.2756)		0.4140 (0.9183)	0.064	−0.053	0.5503	2.2230
Growth in Total Primary Energy GDP Ratio y^2	−0.9167 (1.4636)	−2.0800 (−2.378)	0.8976 (0.9652)		0.2698	0.1786	2.9513	1.5341
	−1.0429 (−0.6824)	−2.0953 (−2.2812)	0.9622 (0.8029)	0.0366 (0.0912)	0.2702	0.1234	1.8515	1.5840

Variable definitions: EEC = 1 if member, 0 otherwise, EUR = 1 if European, AGR = average growth of GDP 1973/84.

Sample: EEC Countries: Belgium, Denmark, Germany, Greece, Ireland, Italy, Luxembourg, Netherlands. Non-EEC Countries: Canada, USA, Japan, Australia, New Zealand, Austria, Portugal, Spain, Sweden, Switzerland, Turkey.

Period: 1973/1984.

and a dummy was incorporated into the analysis to allow for a European effect. The hypothesis tested was that the percentage changes in TPER/GDP ratios between 1973 and 1983 (y^2) were significantly affected by EEC membership (EEC) as well as by being in geographic Europe (EUR), and the results were:

$$y^2 = 0.9167 - 2.3783 \, EEC + 0.8967 \, EUR$$
$$(-1.4636) \, (-2.3783) \quad (0.9652)$$
$$R^2 = 0.2698 \quad \bar{R}^2 = 0.1786$$

Again the explanatory power of the equation is not high. This time, however, belonging to the Community seems to have had a desirable negative impact on energy intensities. The contrast is most marked with the rest of Europe perhaps because both the U.S.A. and Japan had a relatively good record of efficiency improvements. Most of this change would appear to have been due to structural changes in the EEC countries and the movement from heavy industry in particular, a movement unanticipated and unwanted by the Community. Allowing for relative economic growth amongst the explanatory variables does not add anything to the explanatory power of the equation.

Testing the third objective — greater harmonisation of prices for end users is more difficult. Here we are trying to find whether, over time, the dispersion of prices has decreased more in the EEC than in other industrialised countries. A straightforward way of testing this hypothesis is to compute the variance of price at the beginning and end of the period and to test the ratio of these variances against the F distribution for significant change. Table 5 contains estimates of the standard deviations of prices for two products — gasoline and electricity sales to industry within both the EEC and non EEC groups over the period 1979 to 1984. Prices are converted to US dollars for comparability. In the case of gasoline, no clear trend in price variation emerges amongst the EEC countries. The ratio of variances between the beginning and

Table 5. Variations in gasoline and industrial electricity prices — EEC and non-EEC.

	Standard Deviations (σ)			
	Gasoline Prices per litre		Electricity Prices per kwt	
	EEC	Non-EEC	EEC	Non-EEC
1979	0.082	0.157	0.008	0.015
1980	0.077	0.198	0.010	0.019
1981	0.059	0.167	0.011	0.021
1982	0.062	0.140	0.012	0.020
1983	0.078	0.124	0.010	0.021
1984	0.080	0.105	0.008	0.020

F-Test of Ratios of 1984 over 1979 Prices.

	Ratio of Variances ($\sigma_{84}^2/\sigma_{79}^2$)	
	EEC	Non-EEC
Gasoline	1.0696	2.2474
Electricity	1.0137	1.7532
$df_{79} = df_{84}$	10	12
F.01	4.849	4.155
F.10	2.323	2.209

the end of the period is 1.0696 which is insufficient to reject the null hypothesis of zero change. In the "control" group of non EEC countries, on the other hand, price variation tended to decrease over the period, although this change was significant only at the 10% level. Electricity prices exhibit quite a different pattern of variation. In both groups the standard deviation tended to increase until 1983 and then to fall back. The ratio of variances for the non EEC group was greater than for the EEC group but neither exhibited a significant change on the basis of the F-test. A regression analysis of price deviations against time confirmed that there were no significant trends in either group.

7. CONCLUSION

Other aspects of EEC energy policy are not susceptible to testing because of their long term nature. Thus the impact of policies designed to improve the availability of data to decision makers are likely to be long term. Again, the research, development and demonstration programmes on which the Community has spent much of it energy budgets will not bear fruit for many years. It is likely that these will prove to be the Community's most significant contributions to efficient energy provision.

The Community has concerned itself largely with two objectives of policy — a desire to ensure sufficient energy supplies to enable the member states to produce a growing level of GDP and a desire to achieve as great a degree of energy self sufficiency as possible. In regard to the first objective it has not paid enough attention to the functioning of the energy market and prices in adjusting demands and stimulating supplies. Its policies to secure greater import independence have not been sensitive to changes in oil prices. Such policies are likely to come under increasing pressure as the economic justification for oil stockpiles comes into question.

Instead of attempting to prescribe detailed targets for each sector of the energy market, the Community might be wiser to pursue an energy policy more closely linked with concerns of efficiency and equity. One such area would be the structure of the energy markets themselves many of which exhibit significant monopolistic characteristics especially in regard to the provision of gas and electricity. The Commission might also set its sights on the attainment of lower cost supplies by efforts towards establishing freer trade in energy — the trade in gas is a good example. Coal subsidies, formal and informal links between electricity producers and coal suppliers, might well be eliminated in the interests of efficiency. Existing efforts in the information area — collecting and disseminating data on price movements — are justified to some extent by external economies, as are its attempts to promote RD and D projects and these might well be given more emphasis in future policy.

NOTES AND REFERENCES

1. See *Official Journal of the Council (OJC)*, 241, 25 September 1986.
2. Schmallensee, R., "Appropriate Government Policy Toward Commercialization of New Energy Supply Technologies", *The Energy Journal*, Vol 1, No. 2, (April 1980), 1—37.
3. Commission of the European Communities (1974), "Towards a New Energy Policy Strategy for the European Community", *Bulletin of the EC*, Supplement 4/74.
4. "Vigorous action must be taken in order both to guarantee greater security of supply and to prevent violent changes in the prices of energy materials", *Bulletin of the European Community* (1974), p. 7.
5. J. Tinbergen, *On the Theory of Economic Policy*, North Holland, 1970.
6. "Objectives of European Energy Policy", Council Resolution. *OJC*, 149, 18 June 1980.
7. The Energy Programme of the European Communities (1979). *Com*, (79) 527, p. 6. "The damage incurred from an energy supply constraint on economic growth would be much greater than the cost of making over provision".
8. "New Community Energy Objectives", *Com* (85) 245.
9. "Progress in Structural Change — The Main Findings of the Commission's Review of Member States' Energy Policies", *Com* (84) 87, final.
10. "Energy Policies and Programmes of IEA Countries", 1984 Review (1985) OECD/IEA Paris. p. 14. Net Import costs for the 9 members of the EC excluding France were:

	1973	1980	1983
EC	13.0	70.2	41.9
OECD	33.8	263.8	176.6

$billion (US current prices)

The overall increase between 1973 and 1983 of 3.2 times for the EC is substantially less than that for the OECD as a whole (5.2 times).

11. See "Nuclear Power in the European communities one year after Chernobyl" in Energy in Europe, No. 7 July 1987, p. 9.
12. Oil Market Report. International Energy Agency. Nov 1985.
13. The IEA has the following member countries — Canada, USA, Japan, Australia, New Zealand, Austria, Belgium, Denmark, Germany, Greece, Ireland, Italy, Luxembourg, Netherlands, Norway, Portugal, Spain, Sweden, Switzerland, Turkey and the UK. Data is taken from "Energy Policies and Programmes of IEA Countries — Review". IEA. 1984, 1985 and 1986 issues.

European industrial policy against the background of the Single European Act

ELIZABETH DE GHELLINCK

The purpose of this paper is to examine the perspectives offered by the Single European Act (S.E.A.) in the field of industrial policy. The first section outlines the evolution of the European industrial policy. It shows that rather than looking for static efficiency, as it was done in the 1960's where firms large enough to compete with the U.S. ones were promoted, industrial policy has to focus on flexibility which constitutes nowdays a determinant advantage in the competitive game. From the beginning of the 1980's, Member States have become increasingly aware of the rigidities arising from the fragmentation of the internal market. The importance of such a consensus for an efficient implementation of industrial policy is developed in section 2. Arguments in favor of such a proposition appear from the analysis of national industrial policies as well as of European industrial policy. Section 3 considers the impact of the S.E.A., which is a major materialization of such a consensus, on industrial policy. Increasing allowance for majority voting is expected to produce the main effects as far as it speeds up the decision-making process. Section 4 examines the merger control regulation adopted in December 1989.

Special attention is devoted to the producer service sector in section 5 as the competiveness of manufacturing firms depends

P. Coffey (ed.), Main Economic Policy Areas of the EEC – Toward 1992, pp. 125–156.

more and more on the efficiency of the service sector and as the contribution of this sector to the net job creation and to the growth of the G.D.P. has proved to be substantial during the recession. Finally, the conclusion points out that the procedural modifications brought by the S.E.A. are only optional and not compulsory.

1. THE EVOLUTION OF INDUSTRIAL POLICY: FROM STATIC TO DYNAMIC EFFICIENCY

Whilst common policies in the field of agriculture, competition, employment, trade, transport, and fiscal harmonization are explicitly prescribed in the Rome Treaty, no mention is made of industrial policy.

The abolition of internal tariffs and trade barriers and the creation of a common internal market were thought to provide such a competitive impetus to induce a natural adjustment of the structure of productive capacities. The general presumption was that the access to an enlarged market would enable firms to achieve economies of scale and scope and hence increase their productivity whilst at the same time confrontation with producers from other countries would increase competition, drive prices down and favor innovation. Along with this conventional theoretical wisdom, free trade is a sufficient device for an optimal allocation of resources.

On the contrary, the two sectoral treaties — ECSC and Euratom — indicate, without explicitly stating it, the desire to create a common policy. In entrusting to the High Authority powers of supranational management, the member states permitted the creation of a common strategy in the fields of coal and steel. By creating joint research centres and favouring contracts, especially aimed at promoting the coordination between research centres and national programmes, Euratom intended to develop research and to spur industrial initiative in the nuclear field at the European level.

This difference between the sectoral treaties and the Rome Treaty might be explained by the characteristics of the sectors covered. High level of capital investment, high degree of concentration and high rate of uncertainty linked to cyclical fluctuations in demand favour ruinous competition in the coal and steel markets. High levels of capital investment, the importance of the risk involved, the strategic character attached to the nuclear field lead either to underinvestment or to duplication in research projects. Specific instruments intended to deal with these market failures were provided by the sectoral treaties. On the other hand the activities covered by the Rome Treaty are heterogeneous and the encountered problems very diverse. The main problem lay in the differences in performance between the European firms and the U.S. ones which were thought to be associateed with the insufficient size of the European firms. It was widely believed that the integration of the European market would allow the firms to realize the desired scale economies without undue concentration and market power. Hence European industrial policies in the 1960's sought to exploit the link between size and competitiveness by promoting the creation of firms large enough to compete with the giants of the U.S. Weak anti-merger laws, their even weaker implementation and the occasional support of particular mergers by governments resulted in a merger boom which transformed the corporate economy in the 1960's. Today, the largest European firms can be compared to the largest firms in the U.S. and are far larger than those in Japan. As shown in Table 1, this merger boom consisted predominantly of horizontal mergers between competing firms in the same industry.

This led to a substantial increase of concentration in European industry. In 1976, the 100 largest corporations in the EC

Table 1. Merger activity in five European nations.

Country	Period	Coverage	Number of Mergers	Percentage Horizontal	Vertical	Other
Sweden	1946—69	Mining and Manufacturing	1,800	79.8	7.6	12.6
France	1950—72	Manufacturing and Distrib.	565	48.3	24.7	27.0
W. Germany	1970—77	All	2,091	72.3	15.2	12.5
UK	1965—77	All	1,562	74.0	4.0	21.0
Netherlands	1958—70	Manufacturing	1,021	62.4	11.6	26.0

Source: Mueller (1980).

accounted for about 30% of the output and employment, and about 30% of EC exports were internal transactions carried out within these 100 firms. The 50 largest companies alone increased their share of manufacturing output from 15% in 1965 to 25% in 1979.[1] Another characteristic of this merger wave, and more generally of all external growth operations, concerns the nature of the participants. The major proportion of all operations was accounted for by national operations between firms belonging to the same member state. On the other hand, Community firms were increasingly ready to cooperate with firms from non-member countries in international operations within the Community. Two types of factors explain this tendency.

1. The creation of European entities is prevented by the absence of corporate European law: transnational groups which tried to organize themselves at European level (Dunlop-Pirelli, Fiat-Citroen, Agfa-Gevaert, Estel, Unidata) had to rely on a very intricate financial structure and finally gave it up. The only transnational

groups today are those which existed before the creation of the Common Market (Philips, Shell, Unilever).

2. The absence of a real internal free trade area which was already noticed by the Commission in 1970. Despite the fact that the dismantling of internal tariff barriers had been a great success, only industries serving the private consumer benefited from the customs unions whereas industries exploiting new technologies failed to break out the frontiers of each national market dependant as they are for their development on public funds and orders. Preference for national production remains particularly strong and is developed through discriminatory purchasing. According to estimates made by the Commission in 1985, over 90% of public sector equipment purchases are made from national suppliers in spite of the obligation to open national procurement to all European corporations. Hence, . . .' firms will think twice before cutting the umbilical cord and launching out on "denationalized" trans-European schemes. A one-off venture with a Japanese or American competition is a more attractive proposition: That way you make up your technological gap without foregoing the protectionist umbrella and/or the privileges (public sector purchasing, R and D, major export contracts, tax reliefs, financial link-ups, etc.) accorded by the state' (Defraigne, 1984, p. 369).[2]

As a consequence of this fragmentation of the internal market aggregate concentration developed without any similar increase in competition. The merger wave led to the creation of big national champions enjoying substantial market power. Protected by national governments and relatively shielded from the challenges of new rivals, these giants did not feel the pressures to leave a declining industry neither to innovate, and thus were unable to respond rapidly to the shocks which occurred in the 1970's. Substantial changes in the real price of raw materials, technological progress characterized by rapid changes in information technology which affects both the process of production as the nature of the products offered, shifts in consumer demands and major reversals in government policy leading to erratic growth, unstable interest and exchange rates, generate a higher degree of uncertainty. Increasing internationalization of the economy accompanied by changes in the international division of labour (the more advanced developing countries getting a comparative advantage in standardized mass products such as textiles, steel, basic chemicals . . .) put a heavy pressure on traditional export markets and push the industrial countries to specialize in high value-added products. To meet such challenges requires the ability to divert away from traditional lines of activity and to develop techniques and products appropriate for varying factor prices and shifting grounds of comparative advantage. Enterprises in industrialized countries are compelled to pay growing attention to the role played by services in the production process and in the sale of goods.

In such cases, size is not a necessary condition for efficient adaptation to large changes in the economic environment. The development of information technology allows for a flexible type of production based on small-series production. Rapid model changes and frequent new designs become the rule as changeovers of production to new products or varieties are effected without friction and at a negligible cost. Size does not even seem to be a sufficient condition. While being of similar size as the largest U.S. firms and far larger than their Japanese rivals, performance of large European firms, and especially their rates of return, remains in the beginning of the eighties inferior to either of their sets of rivals.[3]

Rather than focusing on size and static efficient, policy action has to favour mobility by attacking rigidities resulting from natural but mainly strategic entry and exit barriers erected by firms in order to maintain their dominance and by governments in order to protect their national interests.

Public actions to replace intra-EEC tariffs by various regulatory and institutional barriers affect particularly the European market. National standards (officially adopted for technical safety or health reasons) for example, play a major role in reducing the substitutability between products from different countries, increasing unit costs and distorting production patterns. Estimates made by the European Commission suggest that the resulting border controls cost the companies about 5% of total transport costs. In sunrise industries where R and D plays a crucial role, national industrial policies have led to much duplication and waste of effort by rival member states and their "national champions", many of them being unable to reach a critical mass, not so much at the technological level but at the financial, commercial and distributive level. In declining industries, restrictions on the contraction and exit of unsuccessful firms by means of government subsidies are the principal source of barriers to exit. In the steel industry, most European countries afforded protection to their producers in order to maintain the existing national capacity. This policy is sustainable only if the capacity is reduced in other European countries but implies that one country benefits, at least in the short run, from the rationalization realized by others. This uncoordinated exit game between national champions involves a market selection process which is slow and erratic and depends as much on financial resources — be they private or public — as on any innate comparative advantage.

The need to achieve the completion of a real barrier-free internal market became acute for the Member States confronted more and more to the inefficiencies of such 'beggar thy neighbour' policies and to the overall cost deriving from the fragmentation of the internal market. It is on the importance of such consensus for an efficient implementation of industrial policy that we shall concentrate our attention now.

2. THE IMPORTANCE OF CONSENSUS FOR AN EFFICIENT IMPLEMENTATION OF INDUSTRIAL POLICY

Whilst at the theoretical level, there is an everlasting debate between those which place their confidence in the virtues of competition to allocate resources efficiently and those who advocate a systematic control of industrial development,[4] it is the compatibility of this public stategy with the agents whom it must work rather than the official orientation given to the industrial policy, which seems to determine the success of this policy. An examination of the different national industrial policies and the European industrial policy in the 1970's offers strong arguments in favour of this proposition.

Evolution of national industrial policies

In all European countries, there exists an extensive set of policies towards industry: industry development is everywhere encouraged with a large variety of subgoals of industrial policy as well as a long list of possible instruments.

On the one hand, the general objective of allowing European industries to effectively respond and initiate the process of industrial change has been translated into goals such as the promotion of R and D development, new technical processes and new products, the encouragement of structural adaptation in the labour and capital market, the improvement of international positions and of the terms of trade. On the other hand, there is a continuum in the utilized tools of industrial policy according to their degree of interventionalism, going from the tax credits, accelerated depreciation and loans at specific rates, to subsidies, public share participation and public purchases.

Examination of these different national policies reveal that the assignment of specific instruments to specific goals is not always made explicit by the decision making center. There seems to be most often various instruments for the same objective and several objectives for the same instrument. Different degrees of intervention in different sectors can be observed with some indusrtial sectors affected by specific measures to slow down or to promote industrial changes while others are relatively untouched. As pointed out by Defraigne (1984, p. 369), 'Since National policies are unable to use the combination of demand-pull and domestic competition (because the national markets are too small), they have to rely on "technology push" and "pick the winners" operations which are much more risky and often fail because they are incomplete'. However, as noted in a N.E.D.O. report (1981), both France and Germany have achieved a similar degree of success whilst their industrial policies are officially overall quite different. 'Germany throughout the post-war period has chosen a decentralized approach, eschewing any formal detailed planning and focusing particularly on R and D, and on building up small and medium sized firms. France, with a comparable level of success, has favoured a highly centralized approach, which in spite of Barre's attempts to reverse it in 1976/77, has probably increased in the last few years. Although Industrial Policy has been largely outside the formal planning mechanism, the approach has been "planned" in the broad sense and has concentrated on particular key sectors and the building up of major national companies'.

Furthermore, a growing convergence of these national policies can be observed. Over the recent years, the German authorities have not only intervened in restructuring slow-growth industries but have also selectively supported high-technology industries, such as aerospace, computers, and other 'national champions'.

During the same period, the French approach has been more complex than merely supporting national champions through indicative planning and voluntarist policy. Underneath the language surrounding French industrial policy, there has been an increasing evidence of a significant shift of policy towards a stronger emphasis on the necessity of an integrated European market, of encouraging a competitive business at the international scale, of limiting the existing protectionism, and of entering into a process of deregulation.

Thus, rather than classifying countries in terms of more or less intervention, it seems more reasonable to argue that there has been a diversity of goals and implementation strategies. What is common to the different national industrial policies is their interventionism; what mainly differs — and rightfully so — is the style. It then follows that attributing the relative health of an economy to its allegedly global, hands-off policy, is inaccurate as is overlooking the activist and successful policy of Japan. What seems to matter is not intervention per se. but the compatibility of the public strategy with the agents whom it must work through. This point has been stressed by the Vice President of the Bank of America, J. Wilson.

'Consensus forming clearly is an important and integral part of any effective industrial policy. Without basic agreements between government officials and business and labour leaders on the overall course of such policy, there is no possibility of success. But, unfortunately, consensus forming is a far more complex task than simply forming a new government agency. What makes consensus forming successful in Japan and some of the European countries is that industrial policy is based upon a recognition of the indigenous factors within the country that enable a consensus to be reached.

The success of MITI in Japan, for instance, is largely due to an underlying relationship of trust between government, labour, and industry. This trust is built upon the mutual understanding that exists between the various groups, the continuous contact maintained by their representatives, and a strong national desire in Japan to maintain harmony.

The French are able to build a consensus on industrial policy because of their strongly centralized political and economic structure, and the existence of a managerial elite that moves readily between high-level positions in government and industry. These graduates of the Ecole Nationale d'Administration and the Ecole Polytechnique provide France with a cadre of top managers, which makes the problem of achieving and implementing a consensus a far easier task than in the United States, where public officials and corporate managers tend to view each other as adversaries. The Germans achieve consensus through their great concentration of economic power among a small number of banks and major industries. German banks own sizeable shares on German industry, and the boards of directors of the banks and large companies are tightly interlocked. Such a combination of economic concentration and interlocking directorship provides a ready framework for consensus formation on broad issues of industrial policy'.

Evolution of the European industrial policy

The necessity of defining a general industrial policy at the European level was clearly and publicly asserted by the Commission as early as in 1970 in a Memorandum of the Commission to the Council, entitled The Industrial Policy of the Community. The objective chosen by the authors was 'to allow industry to derive the maximum advantages from the existence and size of the Common Market' (p. 9).

The way they hoped to establish this industrial policy included the following:

— The achievement of a unified market by the elimination of technical obstacles, the opening-up of the public sectors and the abolition of fiscal frontiers.
— Common procurement of technologically advanced products.
— The unification of the judicial, fiscal and financial laws.
— The restructuring of enterprises through the elimination of the obstacles to the formation of transnational European enterprises, using to this end public credits for industrial development in the sectors of advanced technology.
— The organization of changes and adaptation by facilitating changing jobs, industrial exploitation of innovation, improvement in management of enterprises, and in the recruitment of their managers and directors.
— The extension of Community solidarity in economic relations with third parties, in particular by way of the common commercial policy.

The quarrel concerning the enlargement of the Community, the absence of a political consensus on the part of the Member States on the orientation to give to industrial policy and the insistence on the principle of "juste retour" not only delayed the governments' support to this industrial policy until the Declaration of Paris in October 1972 but led to drop or water down the various proposals favouring more positive actions at the Community level. In 1981, the Commission stressed once more the need for the Community to implement specific policies favouring structural adjustment.[5] Besides measures designed to facilitate product standardization and the growth of truly European-wide corporations to take advantage of Europe's inherent economies of scale, the main proposition of this document concerned the suggestion to add an element of "Community preference" in all cases where industrial development involves the participation of public authorities, such as the setting of technical norms and standard, the public procurement policy, the R and D policy . . .

Even if, since 1973, some progress has been realized among others in the field of harmonization of national regulations, opening-up of national markets for purchasing by public and semi-public sectors by forbidding anu "preference" or reservation for national production and cooperation between small and medium- sized enterprises, the White Paper on "Completing the Internal Market" produced by the Commission in preparation of the Milan summit of June 1985, revealed how much still has to be done to overcome internal market fragmentation. However, the covergence in the implementation of national industrial policies and the consensus around the cost of the shortcomings of the Internal Market opened the way to further progress towards European integration.

Important steps are: the revitalization of R and D policy in 1984, (adoption of the Esprit programme, the framework programme and a number of specific research programmes), the Single Community Customs document in 1984 and the adoption, in spring 1985, of the so-called new approach to technical harmonization.

The major manifestation of this progress materialized in the agreement by the Member States on the Single European Act as early as by the end of 1985. After years of budgetary disputes and lengthy negotiations on the admission of new members, Member States came back to the economic core of the Community's decision-making, as the S.E.A. explicitly adopts the central aim of the White paper: The achievement of an area without frontiers.

The S.E.A. extends the formal competence, and hence its potential to act, of the Community to new areas in the field of research, environment, regional and some aspects of social policy. But the major objective of the S.E.A. is to improve the Community's action by allowing for new procedures of decision-making. Paralysingly slow decision-making resulting from the difficulty to reach unanimous agreement convinced the Member states that the completion of the internal market is conditional on a change in the decision-making procedures. Hence qualified majority voting has been extended to several areas. We shall now examine how the S.E.A. is liable to affect the implementation of European industrial policy.

3. THE IMPACT OF THE S.E.A. ON EUROPEAN INDUSTRIAL POLICY

We have developed the proposition that rather than focusing on size and static efficiency, policy action should favour mobility. As nine-tenths of all industrial policy measures take place at the national level, the role of the Community will hence be that of a coordinator of national policies, of a promoter of cooperation at the European level, and of an instigator of measures favouring the flexibility of the economic structure.

a) *Coordination* of national policies generate beneficial effects in declining industries as well as in sun-rise industries. The control of state aids is of particular importance in this context. The assessment of their compatibility with the Common Market from the standpoint of the Community rather than of a single Member State ensures that public funds are not used to confer a competitive advantage to some firms at the expense of others. Organizing a concerted reduction of capacity in the steel industry (such that investment programmes must be approved by the Commission and must involve a reduction in total capacity) will avoid cut-throat competition between national industrial policies and help to restore a more efficient selection process. In high technology industries, coordination provides a framework for European technical standardization which will allow firms to exploit economies of scale and increase their competitiveness. The abandonment of the sectoral approach to technical harmonization in favour of a more comprehensive strategy offers strong promises in this field. As harmonization is not a goal per se but a means to allow free movement of goods and services, mutual recognition of national regulations inspired by the same goals (safety, health . . .) would increase the efficiency of the decision-making procedure. Rather than looking for unanimity around detailed technical propositions which inevitably hurts one or another national interest, this system asks only for the adoption by the Council of essential safety requirements (or other requirements in the general interest) to which products placed on the market must conform in order to enjoy freedom of movement throughout the Community. However, coexistence of national regulations is not always sensible from an economic point of view. When common standards of production constitute one of the main arguments in the competitive game, e.g., in the field of telecommunications or E.D.P, it remains necessary to harmonize national regulations. The possibility to adopt regulations (and not only directives) would give the Community more flexibility in this field. However, in a declaration the Member States have stated where harmonization involves the amendment of existing national regulations in one or more Member States (Corbett, 1987, p. 262).

Coordination of national policies also plays an important role in the field of public procurement markets which account for 15% of European G.D.P. A radical shift in the behaviour of member states which grant almost all their work to national suppliers is expected to result from directives which force purchasers to treat Community suppliers on a competitive basis. This will throw the market for public purchasing open to cross-border competition. On January 22nd, 1990, the EC industry ministers agreed on a directive proposal to extend these EC procurement rules to four important sectors — energy, transport, water, and telecoms — which amount for more than half of total public capital projects in the Community. A mildly protectionist Buy Europe clause is included in this directive. This clause will allow buyers in these four sectors to ignore non-Community buyers so long as their bids are less than 3% cheaper than the best EC tender or when more than half of the products used are manufactured outside the Community. This clause will be removed if the GATT talks succeed in lifting such preferences worldwide.

Qualified majority voting is allowed by the S.E.A. for all the harmonization measures formerly covered by Art. 100 except those concerning fiscal policy, free movement of persons and the rights of employees. But Member States have the possibility to derogate from these harmonization measures when a vital national interest is at stake. This possibility, however, is subject to prior notification by the Member State and confirmation by the Commission of the validity of the escape clause.

Finally, the S.E.A. states that despite the Commission's proposal that, insofar as common provisions are not adopted by 1992, mutual recognition of nation regulations would become automatic this could result only from a qualified majority decision taken by the Council.

b) The promotion of *cooperation* at the European level takes various forms: Cooperation between firms might be disirable where the achievement of a critical mass is an important prerequisite, i.e., where scale economies and efficiencies due to learning are important or when administrative internal allocation allows better achievement of lower costs and higher profits than allocation by the invisible hands of market mechanisms.[6] This is clearly the case in the field of major R and D projects in the aeronautic industry, in the E.D.P. industry and in the telecom industry where collaboration offers a means of spreading costs and risks and of gaining access to markets. Joint research programmes involving participants originating from different Member States focus attention away from purely national interests and speed up the diffusion of information and the development of a common technology base. A de facto preference to trans-European groups is hence included in research programmes such as Esprit in the field of information technologies, and Race in the field of telecommunications. The setting up of another collaborative framework, Eureka, involving 19 European governments stresses the convergence between the Community approach and the governments' interests in this area. As stated by Shearman (1987), 'European collaboration is on the agenda because governments wish to retain their strategic interests at either national or European level in particular sectors or industries'. However, this convergence has not led the Member States to improve substantially the means of action of the Community in this field. 'Agreement was reached quickly on the various types of Community action (Community programmes, Community participation in programmes of other bodies or of Member States, the possibility for third parties to participate in Community programmes, the establishment of joint undertakings or other structures). However, there was divergence on decision-making. Germany was particularly anxious that decisions on finance should be unanimous. The compromise negotiated provided for unanimity in the adoption of the multiannual framework programme laying down the general lines of Community action, and for the adoption of particular programmes and their implementation. However, the framework programme would go into considerable detail, including the amounts estimated necessary for the Community's financial participation as well as the division of this amount among the various activities. It was specified that Community expenditure in this field would be approved under the bugetary procedure, but that the total amount could not exceed that provided for in the framework programme, thus limiting the EF's bugetary powers in this field'. (Corbett, 1987, p. 250).

In the antitrust area, a more flexible approach has been adopted in 1985 with regard to constructive forms of cooperation between firms. Agreements which favour the dissemination of new technology (block exemption for patent and know-how licensing) and agreements which allow the cost of R and D diminish, to increase the size of risk which can be afforded and save time in the technological cooperation (block exemption which covers agreements providing for joint R and D and joint exploitation of results) are now exempted under art. 85 § 3.

Finally, industrial cooperation is also impelled by a propitious legal environment. Adoption in 1985 by the Council of the Regulation on the establishment of a European Economic Interest Grouping (EEIG) provides for the first time the firms with an instrument of cooperation based on Community law.

c) Measures favouring the *flexibility* of the economic structure include not only the implementation of a vigorous competition policy and of a uniform common commercial policy but also a whole set of interventions creating an environment propitious to the diffusion of innovation.

In the field of competition policy, a major step has been achieved in December 1989 with the adoption by the Council of a merger control regulation. Section 4 examines this new instrument. Section 5 sheds some light on the situation of the service sector in the European countries and mentions some proposals for Community action in this field as the flexibility and the competitiveness of the productive sector is more and more dependent on the existence of an efficient service sector.

4. THE EUROPEAN MERGER CONTROL

Mergers and acquisitions in the treaties

Whilst the ECSC Treaty provides for a systematic control of mergers and acquisitions in the coal and steel market, there is no article in the Rome Treaty which specifically deals with mergers and acquisitions. The European Community and the European Court of Justice have interpreted art. 95 and 96 in such a way as to make them applicable to mergers and acquisitions.

In the Continental Can case (1973), the Commission followed by the Court, considered that business strategies which indirectly exert detrimental effects on consumers through their more or less irreversible impact on an effective competitive structure constitute an abuse of dominant position.

In the Philip Morris case (1987), the Court stated that the acquisition of a minority share-holding in a competing company may constitute an infringement of article 85, when such an acquisition "serves as an instrument for influencing the commercial conduct of the companies in question so as to restrict or distort competition on the market on which they carry on their business".

Through these two judgements, the Commission has obtained power to control mergers and acquisitions. However, this power is limited and not very efficient. Article 85 has a limited domain of application: minority acquisitions with an agreement which provides for an effective control of the target company. Article 86 enables the Commission to intervene when mergers or acquisitions strengthen market dominance and substantially impair competition. This ex-post control creates legal uncertainty for firms and implies heavy economic, social and financial costs if a dismantling of the merger is ordered.

This explains why the Commission, confronted to the merger wave of the late sixties and the emergence of big national champions, drafted as early as in 1973, a proposal for a European merger control. Despite the quick full support of the European Parliament to the Commission's proposal and various attempts by the Commission to modify the proposed regulation, the Council repeatedly blocked this initiative. The 1992 perspective and the corresponding wave of mergers and acquisitions has increased the urgency of this regulation. Consensus on a European merger control was finally reached by the Council in December 1989.

1992 and the boom of mergers and acquisitions

Completion of the internal market by 92 has induced economic actors to adapt their strategy to this new environment. Increasing specialization on excellence activities coupled with a broader geographic coverage induce the firms to sell off marginal businesses or businesses where their competitive position is weak and to acquire companies active in their priority business in other member states.

As Table 2 shows, the number of mergers and majority acquisitions realized by the 1000 largest European industrial firms increased from 155 in 1983/84 to 383 in 1987/88. If national operations still account for more than 50% of the total number of operations, 87/88 shows a sharp decline in the relative importance of this type of operations which in 84/85 or 86/87 accounted for 70% of the total number of operations. This

Table 2. Mergers and majority acquisitions performed by the 1000 largest European companies in the manufacturing sector.

Year	National Operations	Community Operations	International Operations	Total
1983/84	101 (65,2)	29 (18,7)	25 (16,1)	155
1984/85	146 (70,2)	44 (21,2)	18 (8,7)	208
1985/86	145 (63,7)	52 (23,0)	30 (13,3)	227
1986/87	211 (69,6)	75 (24,8)	17 (5,6)	303
1987/88	214 (55,9)	111 (29,0)	58 (17,8)	383

Figures in brackets indicate percentage of total.

relative decrease is due to the growing importance of community operations whose share jumped from 19% in 83/84 to 29% in 87/88. Recent mergers and acquisitions, contrary to the merger wave of the sixties, reflect the growing internationalization of firms in Europe.

The largest firms, with sales exceeding 1 bn Ecu, are by far the most active ones, not only in terms of number of operations but also in terms of growth rate of this number over the period: 92 in 84/85, 268 in 87/88 (Table 3).

Public policy towards mergers

As stated by Mueller (1989), "No topic in industrial organization generates as much disagreement and controversy as mergers ... disagreements exist over (1) whether mergers are adequatly exploited by a profit maximization assumption, (2) whether mergers generate net private returns which are positive, zero or negative, (3) whether mergers generate social returns that go beyond their private returns, and if so what sign do they have, and (4) whether merger policy should stimulate more mergers or try to curtail them". The absence of a general presumption about the

Table 3. Distribution by size of the mergers and majority acquisitions in the manufacturing sector.

	Sales < 500 M Ecu	Sales 500—1000 M Ecu	Sales > 1000 M Ecus
1984/85	62	31	92
1985/86	63	33	108
1986/87	101	31	171
1987/88	61	54	268

Source: E.C. Report on Competition policy, 1988.

impact of mergers and acquisitions on the competitive environment results from the fact that they might as well generate efficiency gains as entail a risk of reduced competition. Mergers may offer more opportunity to exploit economies of scale and scope but at the expense of an increased monopoly power of the new entity. Mergers may decrease transaction costs as more activities are internalized but at the expense of internal inefficiency. Finally, an active market for corporate control might reduce managerial inefficiencies but induces defensive strategies by management which may operate against the social interest. Although mergers and acquisitions could lead to cost savings and efficiency gains, neither theory nor empirical work provide any cast-iron arguments in favour of a presumption that these operations are generally efficient.

Jacquemin, Buigues and Ilzkowitz (1989), propose four criteria to classify the various sectors according to the potential benefits and cost of concentration operations. High growth of demand and extensive import penetration suggest that the risk of reduced competition should be low, whilst potential gains could be expected from concentration operations in sectors characterized by unexploited economies of scale and scope and high technological content. In tailoring a merger policy, the question is how to retain the socially beneficial mergers and their socially beneficial effects and how at the same time to eliminate or at least reduce the fraction of undesirable mergers. This is the approach of the merger control adopted by the European Commission. Major mergers which have a truly European dimension and which affect the state or development of effective competition in the Common Market are condemned unless these negative effects are more than compensated by positive economic results. Let us examine briefly the main aspects of this regulation.

The European merger control

Article 1 specifies that mergers have a community dimension and are thus subject to regulation "when the total world-wide turnover of all firms concerned exceeds 5 billion Ecu and the total turnover realized in the Community by at least two of the firms involved represents a figure in excess of two hundred fifty million Ecu, unless each of the firms concerned realizes three-quarters of its total community turnover within one and the same member state". All these mergers have to be notified to the Commission. As mentioned in Jacquemin, Buigues and Ilzkowitz (1989, p. 55), recourse to these thresholds calls for important caveats. Even for sectors aggregated at a three-digit level, 5 billion Ecu is sometimes quite high in relation to the amount of economic activity concerned, so that a complete monopolization might not fall within the scope of application.

In its appraisal of the creation or strengthening of a dominant position in the Common market, the Commission is required to consider factors listed in article 2 § 1: the market position, economic and financial power of the firms concerned; the possibility of choosing suppliers and consumers; the access to supplies or to markets; the structure of the markets affected taking into account international competition; the extent of barriers to entry and supply and demand trends for the goods and services concerned.

According to Jacquemin (1989, p. 12), some of these factors (economic and financial power of the firms) are ambiguous indicators without any clear economic content. "The overall impression is that the list of criteria for identifying the creation or reinforcement of a dominant position is unsystematic and needs to be fleshed out be guidelines elucidating their content and their use".

Article 2 § 3 specifies when a merger may be acceptable. This holds true if the merger contributes to "improving technical or economic progress or (to improving) the competitive structure within the Common market, taking due account of the competitiveness of the firms concerned with regard to international competition and of the interests of consumers provided that they do not

a) impose on the firms concerned restrictions which are not indispensable to the achievement of the merger, or

b) afford the firms concerned the possibility of eliminating competition in a substantial part of the products or services concerned.

These criteria are rather vague, and therefore give the Commission and the Court considerable discretionary power in a very sensitive domain as mergers often are part of national restructuring processes and industrial policies. This explains why the Regulation provides for consultation of an advisory committee of national government officials before any decision relying on the efficiency defense is taken (art. 18). Contrary to earlier proposals, the regulation does not contain criteria related to social or regional aspects. This could have led to confusion of goals and instruments. However, as the Commission is soley responsible for scrutinizing all aspects of mergers, there is still a danger that the efficiency defense could be interpreted in a way as to become part of industrial policy. The German approach in two steps where the competition authorities only examine the implications for the intensity of competition and leaves all socio-economic issues to the Federal Minister of Economics avoids this danger.

5. THE ROLE OF THE SERVICE SECTOR IN
   FAVOURING FLEXIBILITY OF THE ECONOMY AS A WHOLE

Economic development of the industrial countries is characterized by an increasing share of services in the G.D.P. and in employment. The share of private and public services in G.D.P. now exceeds 50% in the industrial countries and accounts for 55 to 69% to total employment. Despite their importance in the economy, services have been neglected by economists and policy makers. This neglect of the service economy, which has a long history, has many reasons: the difficulties of defining and measuring services, the lack of a comprehensive theory and conceptional framework and the misconception of the role of services in the development and growth process of modern economies. The rapid relative growth of tertiary output and employment is often seen as a destructive process of de-industrialization. Recently, however, various elements led to new attention on the role and significance of services:

— services are a key policy issue in the international negotiations which take place within the current Gatt round;
— services are at the heart of all discussions on unemployment, particularly in European economies, as the service sector appears as the only provider of net job creation during the period of slow output growth;
— services made a major contribution to the overall growth rate of the G.D.P. during this same period. The contribution of the private service sector has been estimated around 60 to 80%.

The composition of the service sector is changing. Next to old and more traditition services such as transport and distribution, new activities linked to the information technology are experiencing a huge development. The most dynamic evolution within production-oriented services, i.e., distribution, transport, finance and business services, is shown by business services. In 1984, their share in the G.D.P. ranged from 12% (R.F.A.) to 17% (U.K.), 18% (France) and 22% (U.S.).

The development of an efficient producer service sector emerges as a determinant factor of the flexibility and competitiveness of European firms. Services, as a means to differentiate products, play a strategic role in the improvement of the competitiveness of European manufacturing firms confronted to the competitive pressure of the N.I.C.s. Extension of markets in the service sector favour the development of specialized firms which may benefit from economies of scale and higher and more balanced capacity utilization and hence be able to offer cheaper services and/or qualitatively improved services. Rising levels of industrial concentration linked with the development of large multinational companies are observed in banking, securities brokerage, insurance, hotels and travel, real estate and telecommunication sectors. Furthermore, externalization of the service functions favours the internal flexibility of manufacturing firms as it is easier and more rapid to terminate a contract with a service enterprise than to lay off their own employees. Finally, the emergence and expansion of production-oriented service sector gives small — and medium-sized enterprises access to a lot of services which were previously available only to large companies.

It is important to note that whilst services are generally classified as being non-tradeable, progress in communication technology now makes it possible to store and transport certain services. Furthermore, there is a rising complementarity between trade in goods and supply of services. Export of goods is often followed by service sales such as training and maintenance contracts, particularly in the case of data processing systems, power generating equipment, commercial aircraft and more generally turn-key projects. On the other hand, engineering firms designing plants in foreign countries will often incorporate home made equipment or materials. The growing financial interdependence of markets and the expansion of transnational service firms (American Express, Sears) or transnational integral conglomerates (Mitsui, Mitsubishi) have also strengthened the link between manufacturing and service trade.

In 1980, service exports (including investment income as payment for factor services such as interest payments or wages to foreign workers) for the industrial countries (except the U.S.) constituted 27% of trade in goods and services[8] (35% for the U.S.). The degree of competitiveness of the producer service sector will hence not only stimulate the growth of manufacturing (and service) firms but also lead to higher exports of services (and goods through complementarity).

However, various factors constrain the development of producer services. Public regulations (public interventions in the trading and contractual freedom of companies made for reasons of equity or efficiency and justified by market failures) and fiscal policy (taxation advantages and subsidies are less accessible to the service sector than to the manufacturing industry) adversely affect not only the development in the national framework but also impede the international trade services either indirectly — by their impact on the competitiveness of national service sectors — or directly by erecting various barriers to trade (licensing arrangements, government procurement, qualification requirement). In the sector of telecommunication and information services, the absence of uniform norms and standards prevents the development of European-wide efficient service firms and entails substantial additional cost for the users. The absence of a real protection of the intellectual property in I.T. also hinders their development. Finally, the quality of the available infrastructure of telecommunications constitute an important prerequisite for the development of the producer service industry.

The development of a global service policy by the E.C. with the aim to improve the competitiveness of the service sector should focus on two axes: the removal of intra-Community barriers to service trade and investment and the promotion of European-wide information technology services.

The creation of a large unified market will improve the efficiency of service providers by allowing the realization of economies of scale and more specialization and will increase the competition in the service sector . However, to achieve this goal by 1992 will require a huge amount of efforts as the actual degree of integration within the Community is much weaker for service activities than for goods. In 1981, the share of extra-Community trade in transport and other services reached 67% as compared to 50% for merchandise trade.[9] One major factor underlying this situation lies in the national regulations which constrain producer services much more than goods producing industries. Regulations in the service sector are normally executed by a combination of the following instruments: public shareholding, intervention in the price-fixing autonomy of the firms, market access and market exit regulations, regulations limiting the freedom of firms to determine the quality of inputs and outputs and the conditions of operation.

The guidelines of the European strategy in this field, as stated by the Commission in the White Paper on "Completing the Internal Market" are the following: mutual recognition of national supervisory regulations as the primary task of supervising financial institutions should rest with the competent authorities of the Member State of their origin, mutual recognition of qualification requirements, non discrimination between foreigners and domestic firms, abolition of quantitative restrictions mainly in the transport sector.

To be able to face the growing international competition by major transnational corporations originating from the U.S. and Japan in the field of financial services, business services and services linked to information technology, Europe has to devote more specific attention to the new service sectors and mainly to information technology services, i.e. data processing, software developments, information services and telecommunication services. These services offer a major growth potential, constitute an important competitive edge in a world market characterized by increasing uncertainty and are a prerequisite for the emergence of European-wide service firms. Europe still lags behind its major partners in this field.[10] The share of European industries in the world market for information technology services appears to be relatively modest.

According to a study published by the Office of Technology Assessment in 1985, European software firms sold U.S. $ 2.6 billion worth of software products whereas U.S. firms had a share in the world market of roughly 70%. Two thirds of all publicly available data bases in 1983 were located in the U.S. and only 25% in Europe; at least 50% of data base services purchased in Europe are supplied by U.S. sellers. The revenues of European telecommunication services amounted approximatively to U.S. $ 42 billion whilst U.S. revenues were estimated at U.S. $ 110 billion. To foster the development of a Europe information technology sector, E.C. has to establish an adequate telecommunications infrastructure which is of central significance to an increasing utilization of I.T. This will be achieved by

— coordinating the behaviour of national administrations which remain the principal operator and standard setting body;
— obtaining transnational public procurement of communication equipment;
— harmonizing standards for communication equipment (OSI, ISDN, Videotex);
— providing for a joint network expansion (Euronet-Dyane, IDIS).

Other measures deal with training and education policies, the promotion of R and D (with a special emphasis on the protection of intellectual property rights in the software sector) and the promotion of non-material investments by the means of fiscal policy.

CONCLUSIONS

How far is the S.E.A. expected to impinge on European industrial policy? By adopting the central aim of the White Paper on the completion of the internal market, the S.E.A. confirms the convergence between the Member States and the Commission around the cost of internal fragmentation and the need to overcome intra-community trade barriers. Contrary to previous propositions made by the Commission, the White Paper has not been launched in a political vacuum. By allowing for increasing possibilities for majority voting in the Council, the Member States recognize that achieving such an ambitious goal requires more efficient procedures. However, this has been done for a limited number of fields. Those where Member States are unwilling to shift to majority voting are the following: fiscal matters, free movement of persons and workers' rights, environment, framework programme and overall level of finance for R and D, monetary cooperation and coordination of structural funds.

Depending on the level of aspirations these institutional reforms had created, the importance of the progress arising from the S.E.A. is differently evaluated. Some authors evaluate it as a "limited piecemeal advance" (Pryce, 1987, p. 273) whilst others consider it as a "landmark for European integration affairs" (Pelkmans and Robson, 1987, p. 183). Information dispelled out the Commission's fourth report on the implementation of the White Paper[11] shows that 142 of the 279 proposals to be adopted by the Council are actually agreed on and that the Commission tabled out 261 proposals. Except for 18 proposals, the Commission has, earlier than foreseen in the White Paper, completed all the work of the proposals. This represents a remarkable progress as compared with the dismal performance in the late 1970's. In some fields (financial services, capital flows . . .), the programme established in the White Paper has already been achieved or is on its way to be achieved. In other fields, where unanimity is still required (fiscal matters, free movement of persons), the adoption of measures in order to complete the internal market still lags behind. Furthermore, delays in the adoption by member states of Community directives in national law[12] prevent these reforms from becoming effective. The implementation of the S.E.A. only provides for the possibility of an increasing use of majority voting, the effective use of these new procedure rules remains uncertain. To what extent will the recourse to majority voting be modified? Will Member States hesitate to ask for a vote and press prolong discussion until a consensus emerges? How frequent will the threat or use of the various national reservation clauses occur? It is everyday practice that reveals the willingness of the Member States to further progress in European integration.

NOTES

1. Locksley and Ward, 1979.
2. See for example, *The Eighth Report on Competition Policy*, p. 185.
3. See the Appendix in Geroski-Jacquemin (1984, p. 358—362).
4. For a detailed presentation of this debate, see Jacquemin (1983, p. 32—39).
5. A Community Strategy to Develop Europe's Industry, Brussels, 23 October 1981.
6. Geroski and Jacquemin, 1984, p. 349.
7. This section deals extensively with the study by Ochel and Wegner.
8. The importance of international service transactions is underestimated because of unrecorded flows of trade in invisibles and absence of statistics on transactions of services through establishments and multinational firms.
9. E.C., 1984, Study on international services.
10. As stressed in the Commission's communication on "Strengthening the technological base and competitiveness of Community industry", presented in March 1985.
11. COM (89) 311 of 20 June 1989.
12. Only 664 measures out of 1007 to be taken by January 1st, 1990 had actually adopted by the member states.

156

BIBLIOGRAPHY

Corbett R., 1987, "The 1985 Intergovernemental conference and the Single European Act," in *The Dynamics of European Union*, R. Pryce (ed.), Croom Helm, pp. 238—272.

Defraigne P., 1984, "Towards concerted industrial policies in the E.C." in *European Industry: Public Policy and Corporate Strategy*, A. Jacquemin ed., Clarendon Press, pp. 368—377.

Geroski P. and A. Jacquemin, 1984, "Large firms in the European corporate economy and industrial policy in the 1980's," in *European Industry: Public Policy and Corporate Strategy*, A. Jacquemin (ed.), Clarendon Press, pp. 343—367.

Geroski P. and A Jacquemin, 1985, "Industrial change, barriers to mobility and European industrial policy", *Economic Policy*, Nov., pp. 169—218.

Jacquemin A., 1983, "Industrial Policies and the Community", in *Main Economic Policy Areas of the E.E.C.*, P. Coffey (ed.), Martinus Nijhoff Publishers, pp. 27—58.

Jacquemin A., 1989, "Horizontal concentration and European merger policy", Working Paper n°8913, Departement des Sciences Economiques, U.C.L.

Jacquemin A., P. Buigues et F. Ilzkowitz, 1989, "Concentration horizontale, fusions et politique de concurrence dans la Communauté européenne", *Economie Eurioéanne*, n°40, mai.

Locksley G. and T. Ward, 1979, "Concentration in manufacturing in the EEC", *Cambridge Journal of Economics*.

Mueller D. (ed.), 1980, *The Determinants and Effects of Merger*, Oelgesschlagere Gunn, Cambridge.

Mueller D., 1989, "Mergers: causes, effects and policies", *I.J.I.O.*, vol. 7, n°1.

NEDO, 1981, Industrial policies in Europe, Oct. mimeo.

Ochel W, and M. Wegner, 1986, "The role and determinants of services in Europe", E.C. internal document.

Pelkmans J. and P. Robson, 1987, "The aspirations of the White Paper", *Journal of Common Market Studies*, vol. 25, no3, March, pp. 181—192.

Pryce R., 1987, "Past experience and lessons for the future", in *The Dynamics of European Union*, R. Pryce (ed.), Croom Helm, pp. 273—296.

Shearman Cl., 1987, "The case for technological collaboration in Europe", *The European*, vol., no 4, pp. 20—21.

Wilson J., 1985, *The Power Economy*, Little, Brown and Company, Boston.

Conclusions

PETER COFFEY

Elizabeth De Ghellinck, in her contribution on European Industrial Policy against the Background of the Single European Act,
stated, "experience will reveal the strength of the Member States'
willingness to progress further on European integration". To this
very important proviso, the editor would add, "but time is on our
side, and, by the force of necessity, the Member States must
integrate further" — recent events have tended to give support to
the editor's optimism.

In the week of 5—10 October, 1987, the Commission made
important decisions about the Common Agricultural Policy
(CAP), seeking cuts in farm subsidies. Unfortunately, the Commission also sought increases in tariffs. Although the author does
not view the use of quotas with great enthusiasm, their use in the
area of dairy products, has lead to a contraction of production
since April, 1987. Perhaps then, we are seeing the beginning of a
reform of the CAP somewhat as proposed by Piet van den Noort,
i.e., "a decrease in price levels or levels of product quotas".

To the editor, these reforms are welcome because they will
tend to remedy the present scandalous misallocation of economic
resources as embodied in the CAP, but, probably more important
still, will improve relations between the EEC and all those countries throughout the world whose traditional agricultural markets

P. Coffey (ed.), Main Economic Policy Areas of the EEC – Toward 1992, pp. 157–162.
© 1990 Kluwer Academic Publishers, Dordrecht – Printed in the Netherlands.

have been gravely damaged by the Community's policy of barely disguised "dumping". In the case of a country such as Argentina, the existence of the newly re-born political democracy is threatened by the CAP.

In the field of the European Monetary System (EMS), decisions taken by the Ministers, in September, 1987, should lead to a greater co-ordination of economic and monetary policies, a freeing of capital movements (implicit in the Single European Act, SEA, as well as in the Treaty of Rome) and a consequent reinforcement of European Integration.

Inextricably linked to the EMS, the freeing of capital movements and the creation of an economic and monetary union (EMU) is the regional question. In his very comprehensive and profound analysis of the whole regional picture in the EEC, Willem Molle observes that the Community in its policy coordination has caused some contradictions, for example, the CAP has helped the richer North European regions at the expense of the Southern ones. Looking to the future, he refers to the observations made by a recent study (CAM 1987) where it is assumed that the internal market will lead to an increased GDP and hence demand — as well as increasing specialisation. This last development may well increase regional disparities. Likewise, the opening-up of the market for public procurement may cause problems for some regions. In contrast, Willem Molle observes, that, in recent years, regional disparities have decreased. He sees this as being partly due to the phenomenon that whilst labour has continued to move from the centre to the periphery, capital has, in contrast, tended to move in the reverse direction. Furthermore, the editor would stress, that, as in the case of the United Kingdom, so, in France and West Germany, capital and new industries are tending to move from the North to the South. More recently, there have been important capital movements into Spain — this bodes well for other Miditerranean countries. In conclusion, looking to the future, Willem Molle, observing the hitherto weak European Regional Policies, states, "some form of European Regional Policy would still be desirable to check, on the European level, the special consequences of certain national and EC policy measures, and to compensate them as far as possible."

Of course, the real aim of the SEA is to create the large internal market in Western Europe that was talked about so much in the 1950's and 1960's — thus enabling us to have a sound economic base from which to compete with Japan and the United States. Here, Competition, Industrial and Fiscal Policies are of paramount importance. Looking to the future, Walter Hahn stresses the large amount of work which remains to be done before the end of 1992. Thus, the very varied and disparate rates of Value Added Tax (VAT) will have to be reduced to two rates, the standard one lying within the range of 14 to 20 per cent — the reduced rate being between 4 and 9 per cent. The harmonisation of the VAT will be no mean task. Then, there will have to be a Community Corporation Tax — which has been discussed for so many years — and which is a matter of urgent necessity if we are to achieve a real 'Common Market' with freedom of capital movements. Last, but not least, are the questions of the harmonisation of excise duties and the Community Budget. In the case of the former, two countries, Denmark and the Republic of Ireland are likely to suffer heavy revenue (and presumably, welfare) losses through harmonisation. The question here (already posed by Meade in the 1950's) is whether compensation will be made to these countries from Community sources. In the case of the Community Budget, the question of its size and possible future resources is likely to become more critical as demands for more active social and regional policies become stronger. Here, the arguments between those desiring increased Community financial resources and those calling for a more efficient use of existing ones are likely to become fiercer.

Elizabeth Ghellinck, examining industrial policy, observes, correctly, that the EEC does not face a problem of size where enterprises are concerned. Indeed, European companies compete very well with American ones regarding size — and tend to be larger than their Japanese counterparts. No, size is no problem, rather the lack of a 'real' Common Market prevent European companies from using their comparative advantage — we have concentration without competition. Hopefully, all this will change after 1992.

David Hawdon, examining the Community's Energy Policy, utters a word of caution about the future. In their attempts to establish a co-ordinated energy policy among Member States, he observes that the Council and Commission would seem to prefer a policy of security of energy supplies rather than one more linked with economic efficiency and equity — this is a critical observation which could bode ill for the future.

FINAL OBSERVATIONS

Events are now moving so quickly that it is both difficult and unwise to make detailed observations about the main economic policies of the EEC and about 1992 and the SEM planned for the end of that year. Instead, the author will make observations about trends in a few key areas which give cause for concern.

First and foremost, competition. The euphoria generated by 1992 and the "Costs of Non Europe" was based on the likelihood of increased competition, lower costs and prices, increased savings and an improvement in the welfare of citizens through greater choice and lower prices. Unfortunately, despite the adoption of the Mergers' Directive, the Commission, in its 1989 Report on Competition in the Community, published on 26th July, voiced concern about the rush of mergers among Europe's big companies which may have damaged competition. In fact, we are witnessing a veritable stampede of mergers and link-ups between companies — both at the national level (e.g. the merger between the ABN and the AMRO Banks in the Netherlands) as well as cross border ones — notably in the food and drinks sector.

There is still potential for increased competition and lower prices — especially in the creation of a European communications market with harmonisation as set down in the two directives in the Official Journal No. L 192, dated 24th July, but, the Commission will have to be very vigilant indeed if we are to transform the EEC into a Community of consumers rather than of producers.

In a parallel area, the compromise agreed upon for the VAT is no more than a compromise — with the proviso that the tax checks will be retroactive and not trade delaying. However, the amount of extra paperwork needed, cannot be calculated. Zero rating will remain, though, in principle, no new ones will be allowed. Tax rates will, in fact, be brought down to the bands originally proposed by the Commission, 14—20 and 4—9 per cent, or held above agreed minimums. This is a temporary arrangement but no definitive agreement about creating a single European tax area based on the origin principle has been made. In fact, little, if any progress has been made and the prospect of more bureaucracy makes the author shudder.

Recent events in Eastern Europe — and especially in East Germany — indicate that the costs of integrating these countries with their West European counterparts may well be much higher than had been originally envisaged. Consequently, this will place extra demands on the Community and national budgets. In turn, an increase in social tensions in both parts of Europe cannot be excluded. Whether or not the adoption of the Social Charter will dampen or exacerbate these tensions cannot be forecast.

Events in the Gulf will certainly give an impetus to the Community's energy policy and reinforce the EEC's moves towards self-sufficiency in energy. Similarly, these events have increased international monetary instability and enhanced the status of the Deutsche Mark and the Pound Sterling. They, together with the monetary union between the two Germanies, have highlighted tensions within the EMS but also underlined the necessity of co-ordinating economic and monetary policies among EEC Member States.

Despite these words of warning, and inevitable disappoint-ments, the author does observe an increased vitality inside the Community, more capital investment, moves towards the adop-tion of a real Transport Policy (certainly a chapter on this policy area will be included in a subsequent edition) and the removal of frontiers between countries. The economies of all West European countries, and, hopefully, subsequently of our East European counterparts, are becoming more and more integrated. Con-sequently, the argument for increased economic and monetary co-operation between Member States becomes stronger. It is thus the question about subsequent moves towards the establishment of a full economic and monetary union which will be examined at the intergovernmental conference which will be held in Rome, in December, this year. The outcome of this conference could well be critical and historical for the economic and political future of Europe.

Index

163

166

Supplementary index of tables

169